Whither Assessment?

Discussions following a seminar, London, March 2002

Edited by Carolyn Richardson

Qualifications and Curriculum Authority

First published in 2003
This collection is copyright © Qualifications and Curriculum Authority 2003
Copyright in the individual chapters remains with the chapter authors.

British Library Cataloguing in Publication Data
A catalogue record for this book is available from the British Library.

Reproduction, storage, adaptation or translation, in any form or by any means, of this publication is prohibited without prior written permission of the publisher, unless within the terms of licences issued by the Copyright Licensing Agency. Excerpts may be reproduced for the purpose of research, private study, criticism or review, or by educational institutions solely for educational purposes, without permission, provided full acknowledgement is given.

Printed in Great Britain.

The Qualifications and Curriculum Authority is an exempt charity under Schedule 2 of the Charities Act 1993.

Qualifications and Curriculum Authority
83 Piccadilly
London W1J 8QA
www.qca.org.uk

Compiled and edited by Carolyn Richardson Publishing Services (cr@publiserve.fsnet.co.uk).

Design by Rob Stephen.

Index compiled by Frank Pert.

Paperback ISBN: 1 85838 501 6

Contents

List of figures and tables

List of contributors

Hugh Burkhardt is a director of the Mathematics Assessment Resource Service (MARS) at the University of Nottingham. He and his colleagues at the Shell Centre for Mathematical Education have developed a research-based 'design engineering' approach to the creation of 'tools' to support high-quality teaching, assessment, professional development and other aspects of educational improvement. ICT has been an important theme in their work for 25 years. They are responsible for the problem solving strand of the World Class Arena project.

Shirley Clarke was a primary teacher, a mathematics advisor and coordinator of the Consortium for Assessment and Testing in Schools (CATS) key stage 1 test development agency before becoming a member of Assessment, Guidance and Effective Learning (AGEL) at the Institute of Education. Her work involves national and international INSET and research about formative assessment. She is a popular speaker whose local and regional courses for primary teachers are always in demand. Her publications include *Targeting Assessment in the Primary Classroom* (1998) and *Unlocking Formative Assessment* (2001), both published by Hodder and Stoughton Educational. She is now an educational consultant and Associate of the Institute of Education.

Chris Collins is an independent consultant, currently providing strategic planning advice to the Qualifications and Curriculum Authority (QCA) on the deployment of ICT in assessment. In recent years, he has undertaken senior ICT management roles for blue-chip organisations, including the London Stock Exchange, the Financial Services Authority and a leading Japanese bank. His interests include strategy development, business process change, programme management, and performance measurement and evaluation. An MBA graduate from City University Business School, London, Chris Collins also has an economics degree and diploma in information science from the University of South Africa. He is an elected member of the British Computer Society and the Institute of Quality Assurance. He was a co-author of QCA's *The Use of ICT in Assessment* report, prepared for the Department for Education and Skills (DfES).

Ronald Gallimore has been Professor (Psychology) at the University of California in Los Angeles (UCLA), Department of Psychiatry and Biobehavioral Sciences, since 1971. From 1966 to 1970 he was Research Psychologist at Princess Bernice Pauahi Bishop Museum and Co-Director of the Hawaiian Community Research Project. With Roland Tharp, Ronald Gallimore also spent 10 years directing a laboratory school for Native Hawaiian children in Honolulu: for this work, they were given the 1993 Grawemeyer Award in Education. He is currently co-directing (with James Stigler and James Hiebert) the TIMSS-R Video Study of mathematics and science teaching in seven nations.

Christine Harrison is a lecturer in science education at King's College, London where she shares her time between training new secondary school teachers and researching formative assessment. She is part of the King's Formative Assessment

Project, whose recent work with Medway and Oxfordshire (KMOFAP) and collaborative work with Stanford University on the CAPITAL project are providing insights into how assessment for learning practices might be strengthened and supported in classrooms.

Stephen Heppell is Director of ULTRALAB, Anglia Polytechnic University's learning technology research centre. He is consultant to the DfES Standards Task Force, the Department for Culture, Media and Sport (DCMS) Creative Industries Task Force and the DCMS Internet Policy Committee. A board member of the Scottish Council for Educational Technology and of Mental Health Media, he chairs the multimedia jury for the Royal Television Society. He is a member of the BAFTA Interactive Entertainments Committee and was a member of the Parliamentary Information Superhighway Policy Forum and of the committee producing the *ICT in UK Schools* report. He sits on the BBC's Independent Advice Panel on BBC Online and is working on various projects concerning the future of television. Stephen Heppell remains a teaching professor and is an external examiner for Trinity College, Dublin.

Michael Kingdon, now an independent adviser, is a former teacher and head of science. He joined the University of London School Examinations Board in 1979 as 16+ Research Officer, becoming Head of Research in 1984. From 1989 to 2000 he worked on national curriculum assessment development, evaluation, management and data collection projects for key stages 1 to 3. He is currently working as a consultant for QCA and the Mauritius Examinations Syndicate.

Daniel Pead is Technical Director of the Mathematics Assessment Resource Service (MARS) team at the University of Nottingham. He has been involved in the design and development of many educational software and multimedia projects including the Investigations on Teaching with Microcomputers as an Aid (ITMA) materials in the 1980s, the 'World of Number' interactive video project in the 1990s and the current problem solving strand of World Class Tests.

Martin Ripley is Principal Manager of the New Projects Team at QCA, which is currently developing a national Baseline Assessment Scheme (for five year olds), ICT tests for the statutory assessment programme, World Class Arena, and tests of basic and key skills. After graduating from Harvard University, Martin Ripley taught in Chicago and Shanghai. Since 1991 he has worked on England's national statutory assessment and test development programme. He managed the development of English, mathematics and science tests for seven, 11 and 14 year olds and created a national system for providing evaluative annual feedback to schools.

Martyn Roads is an independent education and assessment consultant. He spent 11 years in further education, developing and managing vocational programmes, before joining BTEC in 1994. From 1995 to 1998 he worked with schools on the introduction of vocational education into the 14 to 19 curriculum. Since 1999, Martyn Roads has been researching the use of IT in assessment. This has included working with the Council for the Curriculum, Examinations and Assessment (CCEA) and

Edexcel on the Paperless Examinations Project (PEP), which aims to use ICT to deliver 'high stakes' examinations into schools and colleges. Martyn Roads was a co-author of QCA's *The Use of ICT in Assessment* report, prepared for the DfES.

James W. Stigler is Professor of Psychology at the University of California, Los Angeles (UCLA), Director of the Third International Mathematics and Science Study (TIMSS) video studies, and founder and Chief Executive Officer of LessonLab Inc. He is co-author with James Hiebert, of *The Teaching Gap* (New York: Free Press, 1999) and, with Harold Stevenson, of *The Learning Gap* (Simon and Schuster, 1992).

Gordon Stobart is Senior Lecturer in Assessment at the University of London Institute of Education, UK. Trained as a teacher and educational psychologist, he studied in the USA as a Fulbright Scholar. He then became Head of Research at London Examinations at the time of the introduction of GCSE. Later, as Principal Research Officer in Assessment at the National Council for Vocational Qualifications, he was involved in the development of GNVQ. He subsequently transferred to QCA, where he worked on national tests and examinations. He is a member of the Assessment Reform Group, reflecting his commitment to assessment for learning.

Sue Swaffield is a lecturer at the University of Cambridge Faculty of Education where she teaches on Masters and Continuing Professional Development programmes; her research interests are within the fields of assessment, leadership and school improvement. Current work includes the Economic and Social Research Council (ESRC) funded 'Learning How to Learn' project. Sue Swaffield was formerly a local authority adviser with responsibility for assessment, and in that role supported the King's Medway Oxfordshire Formative Assessment Project. She was President of the Association of Assessment Inspectors and Advisers (1999–2001), and remains an executive member.

Kathleen Tattersall is Director General of the Assessment and Qualifications Alliance (AQA). A former teacher, she was appointed Secretary to the Joint Matriculation Board in 1990 and became Chief Executive of the Northern Examinations and Assessment Board (NEAB) in 1992. In 1998 she was appointed Director General to the AQA, which in 2000 became a single body following the merger of the Associated Examining Board (AEB) and NEAB. Kathleen Tattersall is also Chair of the Management Committee of the Joint Council for General Qualifications, for which AQA is convenor during 2002–3, and a Member of the Court and Council of Manchester University.

Alastair Walker is Head of Education Services at the Council for the Curriculum, Examinations and Assessment (CCEA) in Northern Ireland. He has responsibility for all CCEA's output in primary, secondary and tertiary education. He began his career as a teacher in Staffordshire; on returning to Northern Ireland in 1975 he became Assistant Secretary to the Northern Ireland GCE Board. Prior to the formation of CCEA in 1994 he was Head of Research and Statistics. As Assistant Director of CCEA, and then Director of Curriculum and Assessment, much of his work focused on the introduction of statutory assessment in Northern Ireland.

Angela Walsh has been Manager of Qualified Teacher Status (QTS) Skills Tests at the Teacher Training Agency (TTA) since 1999. She has particular responsibility for numeracy and ICT tests and analysis of the national data set. Originally a teacher and then Senior Lecturer in Teacher Training, Angela Walsh was previously Deputy Director of a national curriculum development project. In 1989 she moved to the University of Cambridge, where she worked as consultant and in-service trainer. She joined QCA as Professional Officer for mathematics in 1994 and managed development of the national tests in mathematics for seven, 11 and 14 year olds.

Sue Walton currently works at QCA as the Project Director for a new project developing formative assessment materials for ICT at key stage 3. Previously Sue spent 15 years with the UK educational publisher Heinemann, where she was Senior Publisher responsible for commissioning market-leading paper-based and electronic materials for secondary schools across a range of arts and humanities subjects.

Acknowledgements

Chapter 1: Kathleen Tattersall would like to thank her colleagues in AQA, particularly the Research Department and World Class Arena, for all their help and support.

Chapter 3: Ronald Gallimore and James Stigler would like to thank James Hiebert of the University of Delaware, USA. Any good ideas in this paper, and none of the bad ones, were a product of discussions with him.

Chapter 4: Sue Walton and Martin Ripley would like to thank the following QCA colleagues for their help with this chapter: Tim Oates, Helen Patrick and Rob Taylor.

Chapter 8: Michael Kingdon would like to thank the large number of people from QCA, the seven awarding bodies and participating centres who were involved in the research studies that this chapter draws upon. The work of all of these people is acknowledged. In particular, the author wishes to acknowledge the contributions of Alika Gupta and Nicole Magnier in the Basic and Key Skills Delivery Team, Martin Ripley (Principal Manager, New Projects), and Gordon Dixon of Pannell Kerr Forster (consultant to QCA). Lastly, Michael Kingdon's thanks go to Professor John Izard (RMIT University, Melbourne, Australia) who commented on an early draft of this chapter.

Chapter 11: The KMOFAP project provided the evidence that assessment for learning can work in real classrooms in UK schools and also provided some of the detail that teachers need to translate the ideas into their own practice. The teachers in this project have been the main agents of its success. Christine Harrison and Sue Swaffield also wish to acknowledge the guidance, ideas and support to the project by the others involved: Paul Black, Bethan Marshall, Clare Lee and Dylan Wiliam (King's team) and Dorothy Kavannagh (LEA advisor). Invaluable support and advice has been received from Judy Sebba (DfES) and Kate Moise (QCA).

Chapter 12: Hugh Burkhardt and Daniel Pead are particularly grateful to colleagues in the MARS team at Nottingham and Durham, to the programmers at Vivid, and to Martin Ripley, Jeremy Tafler and the whole World Class Arena team, who made it possible for them to explore such an interesting domain.

Preface

Martin Ripley

Qualifications and Curriculum Authority (QCA), London, UK

IN MARCH 2002 the Qualifications and Curriculum Authority (QCA) held an international seminar, drawing together delegates and presenters from around the world. The title of the seminar was 'Whither Assessment?' and its purpose was to examine emerging issues and trends in assessment.

Themes

The seminar was organised around two main themes:
* the application of technology to educational assessment;
* 'assessment for learning', where assessment is used to improve teaching and learning.

There are other significant themes in assessment debate in England – notably the volume of assessment and its impact on the taught curriculum. There is also some debate about the reliability of assessment for the purposes of public accountability. The technology and assessment for learning themes straddle these and other issues. Technology holds out tantalising promises of efficiency, speed, access, more wide-ranging assessment and more useful information being derived from assessments.

The 'assessment for learning' theme leads us to question the relationship between assessment, learning, the learner, pedagogy and the curriculum. Enabling the learner better to understand the intentions of the teacher and to understand the nature and direction of progress is, according to writers such as Paul Black, Dylan Wiliam, Christine Harrison and Sue Swaffield, a tremendously powerful motivator and strategy for improvement. Assessment systems and assessment tools that take as their prime focus the learner and pedagogy are as powerful, albeit in different ways, to the national systems of assessment that pervade schools in England.

Contents

The 'Whither Assessment?' seminar generated intense interest and discussion; this book pulls together the main issues, ideas and debates arising from it. It seems important to begin the book by looking, in Part I, at teaching, and to ask ourselves what it is about teaching that we might be seeking to improve or change through improving and changing assessment. There is a particular focus on technology: how might its use in assessment have a positive impact on teaching?

Part II develops a theme that has become a major element in education politics in England since the seminar: the use of ICT in assessment. I am extremely grateful to my colleague and friend Chris Collins, for bringing a non-educationalist, IT-industry perspective to our discussions. Chris Collins (I think) enjoys asking whether we in education are seeking to use ICT in assessment because we see it as 'inevitable and inexorable' (to quote Randy Elliot Bennett of the Educational Testing Service, USA) or because we see positive educational benefits in doing so. Part II of this book expands on and responds to that question.

Part III poses difficult and challenging questions about the effect that our assessment systems in England have on classroom pedagogy and the curriculum. I find it encouraging that the chapters in this final section argue strongly that assessment systems can be timed to have a significant and positive influence, both in terms of their content and in terms of the information they generate for the learner.

Thanks

I am extremely grateful to Carolyn Richardson for coordinating and managing all our efforts in writing this book. David Hargreaves first conceptualised the 'Whither Assessment?' seminar and provided me with the license and authority to make it what it was. My particular thanks must go to all members of the New Projects Team at QCA, especially Jon Waldren, Alison Brittan, Chloe Campbell-Follett, Nicole Magnier, Katy Pugh, Gill Williams, Val Bainbridge, George Vassiadis and Sladana Krstic, who have been very patient with me and without whom none of this would have been possible. Thanks.

London, January 2003

Introduction

Chris Collins
Independent management consultant, London, UK

Martin Ripley
Qualifications and Curriculum Authority (QCA), London, UK

Martyn Roads
Independent education and assessment consultant, Maidstone, UK

WHEN COMPARED TO OTHER INDUSTRIES, education – and educational assessment in particular – has been slow to embrace information and communications technology (ICT). The processes followed in the UK to develop and deliver tests and public examinations have evolved gradually from the 1860s, when the University of London set its first matriculation examination. Whilst technology has been brought to bear on some assessment processes, the key elements of examinations remain largely unaffected.

There are a number of possible starting points at which one might begin to think about and debate the future development of assessment. It is the purpose of this book to look at three themes: the effects on teaching and learning strategies of using ICT-based assessment; the potential influence of technology on assessment processes; and how the curriculum and formative assessment may be influenced by the introduction of assessment technology. In discussing these areas, the book also presents the different ways in which technology is already influencing formative assessment, tests and examinations.

Vision for the future

Although a large number of projects, pilots and other ICT-based initiatives already exist, what they appear to lack, if they are to make a significant impact on the assessment and testing industry, is coordination within a common rationale – a vision of the benefits that might accrue if ICT were applied to the assessment process on a much wider, national scale.

Many of the ICT-based assessment initiatives face very similar issues. Examples of these include the inadequacy of ICT infrastructure in testing centres, the need for industry standards to promote interoperability between assessment providers, and the modification to existing procedures and controls to maintain ongoing quality and reliability of tests. A national vision, supported by an implementation strategy, would provide the direction and momentum necessary to coordinate current initiatives, experiences and available resources within a wider industry forum.

Such a vision, which would look ahead to the next 15 years and would begin by looking at learning more generally, could include the on-screen computer delivery of national curriculum tests, public examinations and many vocational qualifications in the UK. ICT would replace most existing paper-based testing and new technologies could create exciting opportunities, not currently possible, to assess skills and knowledge. Tests that still need to be delivered in paper form would be electronically scanned for subsequent automated marking by computer, or for on-screen marking by professional assessors. Assessment processes would become more efficient, computer-based marking would prove more reliable, and the feedback from test results would become increasingly timely and information-rich. This would greatly aid results diagnosis and student motivation towards learning. To support the deployment of ICT testing, the technical environment operated by awarding bodies, schools and other assessment industry participants would be developed to agreed technical standards and data interfaces. This would permit greater flexibility in the tests that schools could offer, and ensure that candidates receive the same high standards of test delivery, regardless of test location.

Assessment at a crossroads

We are now at a crossroads. The use of technology in the classroom is increasing rapidly and there are pressures to realise the perceived benefits and efficiencies that could come from technology in both formative and summative assessment. There is also a growing awareness that increasing the use of technology in assessment will involve more than simply applying it to the existing paper-based processes; its use can bring other benefits to the teaching and learning process. These benefits will include increased diagnostics, which will help teachers to prepare the best teaching and learning strategies and to measure performance of both learners and institutions.

At the same time, we are undertaking more assessment than ever and there are pressures to use technology both to increase efficiency and to improve the reliability of the process. In delivering these requirements, we also need to address ICT's potential to alter radically:
- the teaching and learning strategies employed by teachers;
- the way students learn;
- the styles and types of assessment used, and what the assessments are capable of assessing;
- the whole assessment process and current examination structure;
  and, eventually,
- the way the curriculum is structured.

The three parts of this book begin to address these themes. *Part I* examines the relationship between the use of technology and the teaching and learning strategies employed. It explores both the benefits and challenges that the use of technology presents to the classroom teacher. *Part II* examines the process issues – administration, infrastructure, logistics – that will need to be addressed if significant benefits are to be achieved through increased deployment of ICT. It also looks at several ICT-based assessment projects and pilots that are beginning to identify and address these key issues. *Part III* examines the effects of technology on the curriculum, and how the curriculum of the future needs to change concurrent with the technology being introduced.

Reality or improbable dream?

There is little doubt that technologies will develop that may radically change the way in which we assess learners, in addition to providing many benefits and efficiencies over our more traditional paper-based methods. Over the next 15 years, technological developments should enable us to be even more innovative in their use than is perhaps suggested by the contributors to this book. For instance, who in 1985 would have predicted our current widespread use of the internet, electronic and mobile communications or the computing power of a desktop PC? Change is inevitable and one would hope that our successors in 150 years will not be saying that their assessment models are little different from those used in 2003.

Is all this a reality or an improbable dream? Neither this introduction, nor the book as a whole, aims to predict the future. Rather, the intention is to bring to the foreground the arguments for change and for the greater use of technology. The need for more strategic intervention would appear to be an absolute requirement if education is to gain significant advantage from the deployment of more ICT; actual *development* is likely to be about political and educational intentions, and about constructing a case for change on a national scale.

PART I

Teaching and Technology

Overview

Martin Ripley

Qualifications and Curriculum Authority (QCA), London, UK

As we use technology in the classroom, and as it starts to influence assessment, there are good reasons to suppose that it will also have an impact on the taught curriculum and on what we value through our pedagogy. First, research shows us that students' prior access to and familiarity with computers makes a considerable difference to their success with this technology. Secondly, the attitudes of students to assessments can be markedly affected by the provision of well-designed computer-based assessments. Thirdly, it is possible that through asking students to use computer-based assessments we may be encouraging them to think in noticeably different ways. QCA's World Class Arena project is, in part, designed to develop activities that require students to work in non-conventional ways, to use thinking strategies and knowledge that they are not accustomed to using. In this sense, we might soon view computer literacy as a key element of a student's skill set.

ICT has long been vying for a place as a core subject in the national curriculum for England. That place is now much closer: England now has an ICT strategy and QCA is designing tests of ICT to introduce to secondary schools in England over the next few years. It is therefore important that we should consider *why* we are using technology in our classrooms and in assessment. Are the intended benefits mainly financial and efficiency-based? Are we also wanting technology to affect pedagogy, subject knowledge and the ways in which our students are taught to think? Part I offers some glimpses into the power and potential of technology; each looks at a different aspect of technology and the curriculum.

Chapter 1, by Kathleen Tattersall, examines the relationship between technology, assessment and the curriculum. It asks us to think about the nature of technology and how it is used in England as part of the assessment process. The chapter argues that technology has the power to influence curriculum and learning, and will do so in part through the use of technology in the assessment process. The chapter also shows that education cannot yet distinguish clearly between what it *wants* and what it *does not want* from technology. Even if we know that the road ahead is technology-based, its route is not yet clear to us.

Shirley Clarke, in Chapter 2, describes the difficulties of taking an educational idea, or a part of educational culture, from one country and applying it to another. One of the influences on James Stigler and his team's later technology-based work can be found in Japanese schools: 'Lesson Study' is an intriguingly powerful concept, designed to improve subject and pedagogical knowledge of the classroom teacher. Shirley Clarke's chapter argues that video-based technology can equally well find an influential place in the UK.

In Chapter 3, Ronald Gallimore and James Stigler describe the use of digital video libraries to improve teachers' professional knowledge. The use of this technology has developed following the TIMSS video study of classrooms in the USA, Germany and Japan (Stigler and Hiebert, 1999): teachers are able to look at aspects of their teaching that are otherwise invisible to them – for example, the style of questioning in their classrooms. Digital libraries are attractive and make cultural sense. They do not invade teachers' sense of privacy, yet they provide a strong evidenced-based information library, available across school, local and national boundaries.

In Chapter 4, '"When ready" testing', Sue Walton and I address a more radical concept, and describe how ICT can make its delivery a reality. In considering this form of testing, a balance must be struck between providing the *student* with a more personal assessment system and ensuring that the *teacher* can manage the whole class, with its different ability levels – particularly in the light of the Government's agenda for raising standards. The idea of 'when ready' testing challenges current approaches to testing, and asks why students should not be allowed many attempts at a test, particularly if the analysed outcomes are an aid to future learning. The chapter looks at recent examples of 'when ready' testing and the issues that arise; it also considers its different purposes.

To summarise: Part I of *Whither Assessment?* discusses some of the areas of education that might benefit from technology. Technology might be useful in helping us to do better what we already do; however, if we are to use technology as smartly as other professions have done, we need to be much clearer about how we wish to benefit from its use.

1 Technology, assessment and the taught curriculum

Kathleen Tattersall

Assessment and Qualification Alliance (AQA), Guildford and Manchester, UK

Introduction

THE QUESTION, 'WILL TECHNOLOGY LEAD TO A RADICAL CHANGE in the skills and knowledge we assess?', can be answered in different ways depending on whether it relates to the application of new technology to the administration of tests or to the production of new types of test and student responses.

NEW TECHNOLOGY AND TEST ADMINISTRATION

If the former – machine-marked multiple-choice questions, the distribution of questions to markers following the scanning of candidates' scripts undertaken in 'traditional' examination conditions – the impact on *what* is assessed could be minimal. However, even in a context where new technology is used to improve established procedures, it might be tempting to produce assessment materials leading more readily to responses that can be scanned, or marked by computer. There is a danger, therefore, that assessment will be 'shoehorned' into a technology package for the best of reasons – speedier turnaround of results, more efficient use of markers – which then impacts on the assessment instrument and the learning experience. The backwash of assessment into the classroom cannot be underestimated.

NEW TYPES OF TEST – NEW KINDS OF RESPONSE

On the other hand, if the context in which new technology is deployed is the production of assessment instruments that facilitate both questions *and* responses via computer, the implications for teaching and learning are greater. This scenario gets to the heart of the relationship between assessment and the curriculum. Will the old but forgotten assessment mantra, 'The curriculum comes first', prevail? Or will new assessment approaches spearhead changes in the learning environment? In the UK, the introduction in 1988 of the General Certificate of Secondary Education (GCSE) – where assessment was used quite deliberately as a means of changing approaches to learning – illustrates the power of assessment as an agent for change in the classroom.

We forget at our peril that assessment practices can impact both benignly and adversely on teaching and learning; the history of education is littered with examples of the limitations of 'teaching to the test'. The pitfalls of using assessment unwisely are obvious and call for care on the part of those charged with managing change.

Defining the purpose of learning and its outcomes

However we respond to the challenge of technology in assessment, we need to define clearly from the outset the purpose of learning and its intended outcomes. Bypassing that process means that any assessment system – technological or otherwise – is flawed. Assessment *starts* with learning, *supports* learning and *reports attainment resulting from learning*. The old benchmarks for judging successful attainment – validity and reliability – are important and will remain so even in a technological age. Guarding validity will help to ensure that the style and forms of assessment are compatible with the style, forms and content of learning. Holding fast to reliability will ensure that the outcomes of assessment are a true reflection of the level of achievement that the student has reached.

The impact of technology on teaching and learning

Any question relating to the radical changes in skills and knowledge that technology may bring about in assessment is essentially a question about the impact of technology on teaching and learning. If the skills, knowledge and qualities that are assessed were to change radically *without* corresponding changes in what is taught and learned, there would be something seriously amiss in the relationship between assessment and students' learning.

Awareness of the potential impact of technology on learning explains the concern that too quick an introduction of technology into assessment will have a malign effect, narrowing rather than extending the base of learning, sidelining those skills and qualities that do not lend themselves readily to computer-based assessment. The current question, therefore, is how to deploy technology *without* distorting the skills, knowledge and qualities that we assess in high-profile, 'high stakes' assessments such as those at ages 11 and 14 (the end of key stages 2 and 3) and at GCSE. Is it possible to redesign questions, including their layout, presentation and stimulus material, and assess precisely the same skills and qualities that current tests and assessments address? In other words, can we be assured that as we begin to exploit new technology in assessment, the first generation of computer-based assessment will mimic current pen-and-paper tests? An evolutionary approach, building on existing good practice and taking into account the uneven use of technology in schools, is important. The risks to students, and to the credibility of the assessment process, of mishandling the management of the technological revolution in teaching, learning and assessment are high.

Even allowing for the patchiness of its adoption in schools and colleges and the costs of equipping centres of learning with the necessary hardware and software, the impact of new technology on teaching and learning is likely to increase at a faster rate than any of us can predict. Sooner rather than later, changes in assessment will be needed to reflect a more technologically-based learning society. If the right balance is struck between teaching, learning and assessment, assessment will play a positive role in both supporting and contributing to the learning revolution.

ASSESSMENT FIT FOR PURPOSE

When the time comes to make radical changes to our techniques and methods of assessment, it will be important to remember that assessment must be fit for its purpose. A variety of assessment techniques will continue to be needed. A diversity of assessment instruments will safeguard the range of skills and qualities that are taught and assessed and will neutralise the bias inherent in all assessment instruments.

Types of assessment instrument currently available

The following types of assessment instrument are among those used currently to test the range of skills, knowledge and qualities that learning promotes. Most of them have potential for deployment in a technological context.

MULTIPLE-CHOICE QUESTIONS

Multiple-choice questions provide a ready means of assessing the recall and application of knowledge. In the context of GCSE, General Certificate of Education (GCE) at Advanced Subsidiary (AS) and Advanced (A) level and the Vocational Certificate of Education (VCE), these questions have been sparingly used – indeed, they are constrained by QCA's criteria – partly because they appear to favour boys rather than girls. Other systems use them more widely: for example, the American Scholastic Assessment Tests (SATs). Medical schools in the UK also deploy them to assess higher-order skills in addition to recall. We need to explore their potential for more imaginative use in the assessment of national qualifications in the future. Banks of well-written and pre-tested questions can be constructed, allowing papers to be generated more frequently and thus facilitating tests-on-demand as envisaged in the basic and key skills testing project, for example (see Chapter 8, pages 91 to 101).

SHORT-ANSWER QUESTIONS

Like multiple-choice questions, short-answer questions assess knowledge, recall and related skills in relatively straightforward ways. They are used widely in GCSE and their vocational equivalent. They have the potential for exploitation in a more technologically-based assessment system, particularly if more sophisticated intelligent character recognition (ICR) techniques can be developed. Improved ICR techniques would facilitate computer-based marking of short-answer questions, thus bypassing the need for specialist markers and speeding up marking. It is tempting to hurry down this road, if only because of the shortage of markers, but is technology yet at a stage where we can put more trust in it than we do in human markers?

DATA RESPONSE QUESTIONS

Data response questions might be multiple-choice or short-answer questions, enabling students to use, manipulate and evaluate data. Their continued and more sophisticated deployment in a technological context is clear.

ESSAYS

Essays, which require extended writing, have been regarded for many years as an essential way of assessing 'deep learning', the ability to marshal thoughts, evaluate, synthesise and present ideas cogently. Such questions are used considerably at A level. Their deployment in computer-based assessment systems depends on advances in artificial intelligence methodology. Some would claim that the development of artificial intelligence is already such that essays can be computer marked. However, it is doubtful whether the technique is sufficiently refined to recognise, say, the strength of argument rather than just the syntactic or vocabulary features of an essay. The question is whether such sophistication will ever be achieved or whether, in order to facilitate computer-based assessment, we will forego the wider objectives that essays can assess. Here, in a nutshell, is the kernel of the assessment–technology debate.

PRACTICALS

Practicals are used within the growing array of vocationally-orientated courses, sciences, drama and the like. It is difficult to see at the present time how these might be replicated, but the potential of technology is such that the possibility cannot be ruled out.

ORALS

Orals are used in the assessment of languages, including English. As with practicals, there is likely to be potential here for replacing expensive moderation systems with some technology-based solution.

COURSEWORK

Coursework has, over the years, been publicly criticised by the Government and regulators as being less reliable than end-of-course written examinations. Not surprisingly, therefore, the wider public regards it with some suspicion. There is some evidence that girls do better than boys in such assessments. Set against those factors is the array of qualities and skills that can be assessed as a course of study progresses. Good course assessment demands good specifications and systems of control by examining bodies. It also requires teachers who have the training and expertise to make assessments, to the standard required by the examining body. It is unfortunate that teachers no longer regard coursework assessment as a tool for teaching, learning and their professional development, but as additional workload. However, end-of-course examinations as we know them seem increasingly out of place in an age of ready access to information and demands for instant feedback. Therefore the question has to be asked as to how meaningful it is to continue with formal end-of-course tests as the prime means of assessing students? Greater emphasis on the assessment of work undertaken during the course of study, suitably validated by relatively straightforward tests – comprising, say, multiple-choice or short-answer questions – seems to be ideally suited to more technologically-based learning and teaching. But for the assessment of work during the course to be seen as a credible *alternative* to more formal assessments, some major issues of teacher training and attitudes, public credibility and acceptance would need to be addressed.

Enhancing and augmenting assessment with computer-based solutions

If we want to retain the richness and range of knowledge, skills and qualities that learning promotes, we also need to retain, at least for the moment, the range of assessment techniques that we use currently. Where computer-based solutions replace some of those techniques, it should be because they *enhance* the process, without changing the skills and knowledge assessed. In the immediate future, therefore, it is likely that we will *augment* existing practice with computer-based solutions rather than *replace* it wholesale. However, there is clearly scope to apply technological solutions to assessment, particularly in the multiple-choice and short-answer areas, without changing the learning experience. In particular, the role of coursework in assessing the skills and qualities that technology will undoubtedly promote needs to be reappraised.

Whenever computer-based assessment is deployed, it remains important to ensure that tests are well-constructed against the aims and objectives of the course and the specific skills, knowledge and qualities that the questions are designed to assess. It will also be important to deal with unexpected responses subtly and sympathetically. Students themselves are a major variable, which good assessment practice has to take into account. They interpret the best-designed questions in imaginative and unintended ways. Part of the process of current assessment practice is consideration by the chief or principal examiner of the array of responses to a seemingly straightforward question: decisions are taken to allow or disallow those responses, with appropriate adjustments to marking schemes and instructions to markers. Pre-testing cannot replace this process. Any technological solution to the marking process will need to include a means of accommodating unexpected responses from students.

Guarding against unintended outcomes

ASSESSMENT DOMINATING TEACHING

Some might say that the problems described above can be avoided by simple, unambiguous questions – multiple-choice questions come to mind – rather than open-ended response questions. However, this would be a prime example of the assessment tail wagging the curriculum dog: reducing the range of assessment techniques used would narrow the teaching and learning experience. Although variety in assessment techniques will not guarantee a rich learning environment, a one-dimensional approach would encourage teaching to the test. What is assessed would dominate what is taught.

NEW INEQUALITIES

We must also guard against other unintended outcomes, including the inequitable effects – on boys and girls, for example – of the techniques we deploy. The impact of these unintended outcomes on the reported levels of attainment of students can be considerable. Better handwriting – often, but not exclusively, that of girls – is said to create a favourable impression on markers. Will those with good keyboard skills be the new winners in assessment? And will ready access to computers outside the formal learning context of school or college favour particular social groups over others? Will new social divides open up in the wake of new technology?

On the positive side, technology might well open assessment to groups who were hitherto excluded – students with physical disabilities, for example – thus levelling the playing field for this group of learners.

What will the new society value?

All this assumes that even in a technology-based learning environment, where the pen is as alien to students as the abacus, society will still value skills such as recall and application of knowledge, the interpretation and evaluation of information, the presentation of facts and argument in an ordered and logical way. But what more will society expect of students taught in a technology-rich environment? How might skills and knowledge change? How relevant will a subject-based curriculum continue to be? Will future learning be constructed around generic skills rather than subjects?

These questions prompt others, such as:

- *Will rote learning continue to be relevant in an age of ready access to knowledge?* Innovative question types and access to reference and case-study materials on computer might facilitate the assessment of higher order skills of application of knowledge, interpretation and synthesis rather than – or in addition to – recall.

- In an age of computer aids, *will spelling, punctuation and grammar* (for which there are marks in all GCSE subjects), *or the quality of language* (which A level assesses) *continue to be valued?*

- *Will the use of computers replace basic numerical skills?* In mathematics, we seem to be ambivalent about the use of calculators, wanting to retain the old basic skills as well as to encourage better use of technological tools. Is it realistic to expect students to demonstrate attainment on both fronts?

- *What new possibilities will technology open up for learning?* Problem solving, for example, has long been valued as a skill and there has been a lengthy debate about how to determine what it means and how to assess it. Is it generic or contextually based? What about critical thinking, or the theory of knowledge or logic?

- *Will the new technology present a threat or an opportunity to individual subject areas?* The focus on generic skills and qualities that new technology makes possible might signal the end of the subject barriers, which some would argue are an impediment to learning. All subject specialists across the curriculum will need to ask themselves what subject-specific knowledge and skills can be better targeted by computer-based assessment and what subject-specific knowledge and skills might be redundant in a technological environment? Wider access to knowledge and information should open up new and interesting ways of learning in, for example, subjects like history or geography – and this ought to be reflected in assessment.

• *Will the focus shift from end-of-course assessment to assessment during the course*, with computer-based tests confirming teacher judgement?

World Class Arena

AQA, in partnership with Doublestruck and QCA, is currently developing World Class Tests, which point the way forward on some of these fronts. There is some great innovative work being done in this context, including developing techniques to assess problem solving, which is as exciting to the developers as it is to the students who are taking the tests. It is hoped that the skills and knowledge of these learners are being challenged and extended through these innovative tests.

The World Class Tests and other computer-based assessments will facilitate the tailoring of courses to individual needs, with learners progressing at their own pace, as heralded in the Government's Green Paper of February 2002, *14-19: Extending Opportunities, Raising Standards* (GB.DfES, 2002). If the proposals in the Green Paper come about, there is likely to be a greater call for on-demand assessment. A technological solution to the production and provision of tests will speed up the assessment process and make more efficient use of that scarce resource, the marker. It might also provide formative feedback to teachers and students from the analysis of student performance on the tests. Used alongside assessment during the course, this could be a powerful teaching and learning instrument.

Conclusion

There is no doubt that we are at a crossroads in teaching, learning and assessment. We think we know that the road signposted 'Technology' is the right one to take, but we are not absolutely sure if following it will be as straightforward as it appears on the map. There are likely to be some unforeseen difficulties once we have embarked on the journey. What is important, however, is that all the different strands of education make the journey together, since we are all interdependent. The question, 'Whither assessment?', only has meaning in the wider context of education. We must harness assessment to the curriculum and the curriculum to the needs of individuals. Technology used wisely will help us to fulfil that objective.

The suggestions made and the views expressed in this chapter are the author's own and do not necessarily represent those of the Assessment and Qualifications Alliance.

2 New visions for improving teaching: an introduction to the work of Gallimore, Stigler and Hiebert

Shirley Clarke
Associate of the Institute of Education, University of London, London, UK

Introduction

THIS CHAPTER INTRODUCES the work of Ronald Gallimore and others from the University of California, Los Angeles (UCLA), in creating a 'bottom-up' interactive professional development tool via video technology and the internet; their work is described in more detail in Chapter 3. The concept that they have developed was influenced by the educational ideas and practices of Japanese professional development known as 'Lesson Study', adapted for a United States and world context. Teachers are now provided with a unique and powerful opportunity to pursue the ideal of creating their own effective change, as a result of watching, analysing, interacting with and being part of action research linked to taped lessons.

Background

THE TEACHING GAP

It seems to be generally agreed that there is a gap between the teaching needed to reach rising educational expectations and the practices teachers are accustomed to using (Black and Wiliam, 1998b; Stigler and Hiebert, 1999). The reasons for the gap are:

- new standards involve changing expectations for, and of, teachers;
- many teachers have never seen, or even imagined, the teaching needed to fulfil the greater expectations;
- there is no alignment between teacher development and new expectations, particularly in the US;

• it is difficult to implement and achieve changes in teaching.

Over the years, across the western world, policymakers have tended to use similar strategies to try and improve teaching (for example, they have increased salaries, made changes to the curriculum, and so on), but to little effect.

There are problems inherent in policymakers alone determining a course for teacher improvement for the following reasons:

• change is generally slow and incremental, whereas policymakers tend to want 'quick fixes';
• while the emphasis is on teachers rather than teaching, lasting change does not occur;
• 'top-down' models of professional development do not work – teachers tend to pay lip service to them, but carry on with their existing practice;
• if teachers cannot 'see' the desired practice and understand what is possible, improvement is inaccessible, because descriptions of practice rely on a consistent interpretation of terms and hypothetical models;
• cultural traditions and habits act as a 'racial memory', influencing teachers' style of teaching and beliefs about learning – they use 'teaching scripts'.

Lessons learnt from Japanese education

A significant text in challenging the assumptions of American educational practice is *The Teaching Gap* (Stigler and Hiebert, 1999). The book is based on the Third International Mathematics and Science Study (TIMSS) Video Study (Stigler *et al.*, 1999), which dramatically illustrates why it is so hard to introduce new teaching practices. The TIMMS research team conducted a video survey of nationally representative samples of mathematics lessons for 13 and 14 year old students in the US, Germany and Japan. After months of watching the tapes, the team concluded that it was possible to identify cultural 'teaching scripts' in each country: ways of teaching that are instinctive, based on the norms of the culture and memories of childhood education. The example given in the book to illustrate a cultural script is the family dinner. We participate in events such as these without realising all the aspects that are taken for granted. We all come to the table and begin eating at about the same time. We would be surprised to be given a menu or presented with a bill at the end of the meal. Teaching scripts are the same: we begin school with knowledge about what will take place in that setting, even though we have never been to school before: the norms are 'embedded'. The point here is that the teaching script is instinctive: it is little wonder that it is difficult to initiate real and lasting change in the classroom.

DIFFERENCES IN EDUCATIONAL PRACTICE

The TIMMS video studies focused on lessons in America, Germany and Japan. The clearest contrast seen was between America and Japan, where the practices are very different. Some of the starkest differences reported between US and Japanese methods are described in Table 2.1 (see page 17).

Table 2.1: *Contrasting features of education in the USA and Japan*

	USA	JAPAN
Lesson organisation	US teachers organise lessons by introducing a procedure and terms; students practise this for the rest of the lesson.	Japanese teachers begin lessons by stating learning objectives and previous learning about the topic. Next, they give students an open-ended problem to solve in their own ways; their methods are then shared, with input from the teacher. The lesson concludes with a plenary session, in which learning is developed and consolidated. 'Drill and practice' is still used, but there is always a motive – usually connected with a later open-ended task.
Views on mixed ability	US teachers see differentiation as a problem.	Japanese teachers see mixed ability as a gift.
The use of overhead projectors and chalkboards	US teachers tend to use an overhead projector for teaching points, turning it off when they want students to listen or work; they see the projector as a focus for attention and a motivational tool.	Japanese teachers use a chalkboard as a continuous record of a lesson, to which students have constant access. They see learning as the greatest motivational tool.
Structure of the school day	US students sit for many hours without a break.	School days are longer but each lesson is followed by a short playground break.
	Most US lessons are continually interrupted.	Japanese lessons are never interrupted – the lesson is seen as sacrosanct.

CULTURAL DIFFERENCES

The team also discovered many cultural differences – in, for example, parental attitudes to education. In Japan, even the poorest homes have a desk for each child, whereas in US homes the adults' needs take priority. Interestingly, the authors of *The Learning Gap* (Stevenson and Stigler, 1992), dispel the myth that the Japanese system of education leads to high suicide rates and involves parental pressure. They claim that, although pressure builds during the high school years, when concerns about university exams intensify, such pressure is not evident in pre-school or elementary school settings. The idea that teaching methods in Japan stress rote learning is inaccurate, as illustrated by the many videos of mathematics lessons in Japanese schools. Parents in Japan intensify their interest in their children's academic achievement as the children get older, with an expectation that the pre-school years should be confined to play and the development of social skills. American parents apply pressure to their children from the beginning, generally losing interest as children grow older, believing that the school should become more responsible for student achievement.

The Japanese model of teaching seems totally inaccessible to American teachers, because there is no way of them seeing what is possible in first-hand terms, and cultural scripts are heavily embedded. Methods are dismissed as being inappropriate for US settings. Whilst there are talented teachers in the US, their gifts are not disseminated effectively to others.

The UCLA team looked closely at the Japanese model of teacher development for inspiration and discovered that the main source of teacher development was 'Lesson Study'.

'LESSON STUDY'

Although there are many variations of 'Lesson Study' throughout Japan, the following description serves to outline the basic processes involved.

Focus

Teachers, in groups of approximately five, are given (or decide on) a learning objective focus. This could be a specific concept (for example, finding percentages) or a broader objective (for example, encouraging child autonomy). Over about three months, taking an hour or two a week, the teachers research the objective, finding out more about the concept itself and how others might have taught it.

Planning

The team plans a lesson, in great detail, identifying the responses that students might have at different stages through the lesson, how these should be addressed if they occur, and what should be done to further the learning throughout. The key elements of the planning involve decisions concerning:

• the problem with which the lesson should begin, including the exact wording/numbers to be used;
• the resources students will be given;
• the anticipated solutions, thoughts and responses students might encounter;
• appropriate questions to ask during the lesson, to promote thinking and guide those with misconceptions;
• how to use the space on the chalkboard;
• how to divide up the lesson, allocating appropriate timings;
• how to handle individual differences between students;
• how to end the lesson (seen as a key moment in which student understanding can be advanced).

Lesson

The lesson takes place, often with an audience, and the team takes notes throughout, focusing on whether the intended learning has taken place.

Analysis–rescheduling–final analysis

The lesson is discussed and analysed – and subsequently rewritten, in the light of the first experience. The lesson is then rescheduled, takes place for a second time and observed again. Finally, a further analysis takes place, often followed by writing-up of the lesson.

A summary of aims

The aim of the Lesson Study process is that teachers should benefit more from the process of research, collaborative planning, analysis and discussion than from the end product of a model lesson for one small area of the curriculum. The aim is not to build a bank of perfect lessons, which are then used as a script, although the published lessons are used for future Lesson Study research. The idea is that this kind of teacher involvement will lead to effective and lasting change in teaching because the models of good practice are experienced by teachers at first hand. The processes the teachers engage in throughout the 'Lesson Study' period enable them to apply their expertise to other lessons and subjects. Simply spending time on this 'overplanning', for instance, at the beginning of the process, enhances teachers' knowledge and understanding. The planning stage includes research about the concept, which must increase teachers' subject expertise, but the discussion about the questions to ask, the possible student responses, and how they might be dealt with focuses on the very heart of the teacher's craft or 'guild' knowledge. Effective questioning was identified as one of the significant elements of formative assessment as a result of the substantial trawl of studies involving formative assessment carried out by Black and Wiliam in 1998. It is the language used in lessons that appears to have the greatest impact on student achievement, yet the policymaker emphasis has tended to dwell on improving teacher subject knowledge alone. Policymakers perhaps have their own cultural images of teaching, encapsulated in the many 'back to basics' initiatives.

It is important to say, at this point, that many of the US researchers and Japanese teachers thought that the main aim *was* to create a store of perfect lessons to fit the agreed curriculum. One of the main recommendations in *The Teaching Gap* is that there is a need for a national curriculum that provides a basis for the selection of learning objectives and shared goals.

Teachers involved in Lesson Study see themselves as contributing to the development of knowledge about teaching as well as to their own professional development, so their self esteem and sense of self-worth is enhanced – a vital missing element in today's UK educational climate.

Developing a 'western' equivalent of Lesson Study

PRINCIPLES FOR GRADUAL IMPROVEMENT

Stigler and Hiebert developed six principles for gradual, measurable improvement, as a result of their analysis of the different cultural scripts. These are briefly summarised below, and described in detail in Chapter 3 (see pages 28 to 31).

1. Improvement has to be continual, gradual and incremental

This is a truth that is in stark conflict with today's climate, where education is often a political tool, with short-term 'quick fixes' the only acceptable way forward for policymakers.

2. Maintain a constant focus on student learning goals

While the focus is on activities, the result is an 'activity culture'. If the focus of development is the fulfilment of the learning objectives, the task becomes the means and not the end, with a clear implication that it is the modification of subsequent teaching and activity that will enable goals to be met.

3. Focus on teaching, not teachers

Instead of targeting the competency of teachers, we need to develop effective methods of teaching. Recruiting highly-qualified teachers will not result in steady improvement as long as they continue to use the same scripts. It is the scripts that must be improved.

4. Make improvements in context

The model for improvement needs to come from the grass roots, embedded in real classroom contexts rather than in hypothetical ideas.

5. Make improvement the work

Ideas need to be 'action researched' by working teachers, who try them in different contexts, experiment, share findings and modify and take ownership, as with my own continuing action research about formative assessment – take the research principles and get teachers to find out what it looks like in the classroom (Clarke, 2001).

6. Build a system that can 'learn' from its own experience

When good teachers retire, their knowledge and expertise tends to retire with them. We need to find a way to harness the knowledge base to support change, to build a system with a memory – a means of accumulating the experiences and insights of teachers.

The next step was to find a way of applying these principles in a western context.

DESIGNING A 'KNOWLEDGE BASE'

As a result of Stigler and Hiebert's fascinating discoveries, the UCLA team embarked on creating a version of Lesson Study that could fit the western culture. They focused on video technology as the tool that would enable teachers to be involved in both action research and professional development. The Glenn Commission of 2001, looking at the role of technology in education, stated that:

> *A dedicated Internet Portal must be available to teachers so that they can make use of and contribute to an ever-expanding knowledge base.*
> *(National Commission on Mathematics and Science Teaching for the 21st Century, 2001)*

It also recommended that:
- search engines should be keyed to standards (learning objectives) and curriculum frameworks;
- curriculum and software developers, publishers and academics should collaborate with teachers in generating resources and tools;
- local school systems should provide access to the internet portal.

Key features

The UCLA team began with some principles for a new, robust, accessible form of professional development. It decided that a professional 'knowledge base' for teachers would need to:
- be accessible to teachers;
- be accurate and verified;
- use rich resources that linked to vivid images of alternatives.

Professional development would need to be robust: long-term, site-based and collaborative; it would involve teachers in an active (as opposed to passive) role and would also be coherently integrated into existing efforts.

It is clear that teachers need models of excellence, but the suggested 'perfect' image could simply alienate teachers. The programme would need to involve real, believable teachers in authentic classroom settings, where the aim would not be to illustrate the perfect lesson, but instead to provide a platform for analysis and discussion.

Design principles

The team developed six key design principles for the development of a professional knowledge base. It would need to:

- be linked to practice and aligned with educational content;
- be detailed, concrete and specific to teachers' units of analysis (for example, lessons);
- integrate multiple kinds of knowledge;
- be public, a product of collaboration, and be represented in a format that could be easily communicated to teachers;
- provide a mechanism for verification and improvement;
- be stored and shared.

Clearly, if a product were to be produced for nationwide use, it would need to be cheap, easy to learn, use and navigate, involve active analysis and learning opportunities and link specific practices in video to curriculum objectives or standards, lesson plans and student work. It would also need online learning, coaching and mentoring facilities.

LessonLab

LessonLab was created in 1998 to unite this and other research on teaching and teacher learning with software and program development dedicated to the improvement of teaching. Its current research programme includes the TIMSS–R Video Study. LessonLab has built the largest video database of teaching in the world, containing over 2,000 hours of video collected from mathematics and science classrooms in seven nations.

In 2001, LessonLab launched a software platform to support the development and implementation of innovative, case-based professional learning programs. This allows teachers to study and discuss videos and other artefacts of classroom practice face to face and over the internet.

The LessonLab software is described as:

An integrated platform for creating and delivering case based content in an interactive format over the web. This technology incorporates a synergistic mix of streaming video, user discussions, supplemental materials, expert commentary and personal learning tools to create an enriching professional development experience. The platform consists of three components: 'Viewer', the core user interface for interacting with cases in the digital libraries; 'Builder', the application for creating content for the digital libraries; and the digital libraries themselves that form a scalable repository for case materials.

(See www.lessonlab.com)

VIEWER

At the heart of the software is the 'Viewer'. This is the substitute for 'Lesson Study'. Instead of planning and conducting a lesson – something that would cause enormous time management problems for western teachers (not to mention union action) – lessons are viewed on the internet. The lessons are set up in a format that allows for different kinds of interaction and could easily be used as an interactive professional development tool in, say, staff meetings or professional training days.

The video lessons are subtitled and time coded. The lesson takes place on the left-hand side of the screen, while the rest of the screen is used for various other purposes.

Key features

'Viewer' has translated and developed the 'Lesson Study' model in the following ways.

• A *table of contents* can be viewed, which allows teachers to jump to any section of a lesson (for example, 'She says the learning objective is ... Let's skip to the plenary and see how she rounds off the lesson').

• Each lesson has a *complete transcript*, which can be retrieved and used for staff discussion and analysis at any time (for example, 'Let's look at the section where the teacher asked the child what he thought the answer would be and listen to the dialogue that ensues ...')

• Each lesson has *associated items*: lesson plans, handouts, student work, presentations, video interviews and web links (for example, 'Look at the plan … How well do we think the activity matches the learning objective? How could we improve this student handout?')

• There is a vehicle for teachers to create their own *commentary* on a time-linked section of a lesson, to add to past comments made by other users. This store of analytical comments is particularly exciting in encouraging teachers to be action researchers.

BUILDER

'Builder' is the platform for creating the digital library of videoed lessons, and enables teachers to slot their video material into a form in which 'Viewer' can be used. Its strength is that it does not rely on outside consultants or technology experts.

THE VISION

The LessonLab team was convinced that 'Lesson Study' in its pure Japanese form would not be appropriate or applicable in the United States, because of time management issues and the traditional lack of anything that involved in-depth, long-haul involvement of teachers in analysis of their own and, more importantly, others' practice.

Video technology emerged as the vehicle best suited for enabling teachers to 'see' real practice that would develop their own. However, simply presenting video material to teachers is fraught with problems. Viewers often believe that the on-camera teacher is acting, or that the situation is not realistic – as, for example, in the UK Literacy Hour videos in which only small groups of children were seen, leading teachers to wonder what was happening to the rest of the class. Without a specific focus, viewers are easily distracted by superficial features, such as the on-camera teacher's methods of control, and the potential and power of the video is lost.

The LessonLab software was produced with the teacher as an interactive action researcher in mind. Professional development notes, or ways in which the software could be explicitly used, would be an added bonus, but the tools make clear what is possible *within* teachers' own schools, as a basis for analytic staff meetings, and *between* schools through the commentary sections and other elements.

The vision focuses on the model of slowing down teaching to make it visible. Following the Lesson Study model, the materials can be used to analyse both the planning stage and classroom practice, and then reflect on the effectiveness of that practice in light of the original objectives.

Endnote

During visits to the United States, I spoke to people who have dabbled in Lesson Study in its original form, attempting to recreate the same model. It has been seen as a very useful process but largely marginalised because of the time needed and the view that the curriculum is too vast to spend so much time on such minute detail. Alas, the point has sometimes been missed, that the involvement in one single Lesson Study would enable a teacher to develop skills that could be applied to future contexts. However, a useful point made to me was that if Lesson Study is conducted within a school in isolation, it can lead to a 'recycling' of the participants' lack of subject knowledge – so an outside subject expert is nearly always necessary in the planning meetings. The strength of LessonLab is that it provides the external expertise by being accessible to all users, so I see the action research element as the most powerful tool in this software.

Interestingly, it was pointed out to me that the Japanese would completely dismiss the use of video technology, because the lessons viewed are not live – the videographer/editor potentially compromising the essence of the teacher/student interaction. They would argue that the proximal event is altered through virtual transcription: one can only see one thing at a time, not all the children are visible and there is no substitute for 'live' experience. With Lesson Study, teachers have to plan a real lesson and carry it out, whereas with LessonLab the entire experience can be carried out as a subjective viewer – analysing, admittedly, but without the benefit of the real experience and the thinking needed for the unexpected 'here and now'.

However, with such a powerful, 'bottom-up' model of teacher development on offer, it would be madness not to at least attempt to introduce it into a different culture, in a form that is accessible and acceptable within the constraints and realities of the educational contexts of our worlds. Perhaps the ideal scenario would be one in which LessonLab is combined with some small-scale opportunities for teachers to plan in detail and then conduct and analyse lessons.

In conclusion, the following words from the authors of *The Teaching Gap* encapsulate the vision of the future for improving teaching:

The star teachers of the twentieth century have been those who broke away from the crowd and created different and unusual methods of teaching. They distinguished themselves by being different, by leaving the standard practice behind. They gained fame by rising above the routine and showing the effectiveness of alternative forms of teaching. Although these efforts won the applause of educational critics, they did not have much effect on standard practice.

The star teachers of the twenty-first century will be those who work together to infuse the best ideas into standard practice. They will be teachers who collaborate to build a system that has the goal of improving students' learning in the 'average' classroom, who work to gradually improve standard classroom practices. In a true profession, the wisdom of the profession's members finds its way into the most common methods. The best that we know becomes the standard way of doing something. The star teachers of the twenty-first century will be teachers who work every day to improve teaching – not only their own but that of the whole profession.
(Stigler and Hiebert, 1999)

3 Closing the teaching gap: assisting teachers to adapt to change

Ronald Gallimore
University of California, Los Angeles, USA

James Stigler
LessonLab, Santa Monica, USA

Introduction

THERE IS A GAP BETWEEN the teaching that is needed to reach rising educational expectations and the practices that teachers are accustomed to using (Black and Wiliam, 1998b). In the US, it is increasingly recognised that achievement gains to match rising standards depend on the improvement of teaching (Lampert, 2001; National Commission on Mathematics and Science Teaching for the 21st Century, 2001; Stigler and Hiebert, 1999). This is hardly surprising, since all plausible theories of action identify teaching as the final common pathway connecting curriculum reforms to student outcomes.

How to improve teaching

Many believe that improved teaching will follow structural reforms, for example:
- higher initial salaries and differentiated pay based on merit;
- an increase in the ratio of 'content-based' to 'method-based' courses for teachers in training;
- higher academic standards in teacher preparation;
- broadening of the recruitment pool to include those from non-traditional sources, such as retired military and technical workers.

Optimism that these changes will improve teaching can only be based on the mistaken belief that these ideas are new and untried. Although they were writing about an earlier wave of reform set in motion in the early 1980s, what Sarason and his colleagues noted then is still true today (Stigler and Hiebert, 1999):

> ...*[American reformers] fail to realize that everything being said and proposed was said, proposed, and acted upon earlier as a reaction to the narcissistic wound experienced by [US] society when the Soviet Union orbited the first sputnik in 1957.*
>
> *(Sarason, 1983, p.4)*

> ...*[what is] recommended for improving the preparation of teachers has been recommended countless times in the past without discernable effect, e.g., better grounding in specific subject matter and the arts and sciences generally, better supervision, more in-service and continuing education opportunities, stricter and more objective standards for judging teacher performance and competency, and greater and material recognition of superior teachers.*
>
> *(Sarason, Davidson and Blatt, 1986, pp.vii-ix)*

THE BENEFITS OF PROFESSIONAL DEVELOPMENT

Happily, many now recognise that structural reforms have limited effects unless the intended changes are implemented in classrooms, and that implementation depends on robust professional development. Teachers are receiving site-based, long-term professional development in grade-level or departmental contexts (Darling-Hammond and Sykes, 1999; Loucks-Horsley *et al.*, 1998). This training covers how to implement standards-based instruction, and how to develop and analyse student performance assessments. Some teachers are given time during the working week to collaboratively develop and try out lessons, then revise and re-teach them. Teacher response to these opportunities is positive (Garet *et al.*, 2001); this time, perhaps intended reforms may actually be implemented in classrooms.

Even with new professional development opportunities, improvements in teaching will not be easily achieved. Despite many attempts to change it, teaching in the 1990s differed little from the instructional practices described decades earlier by Rice (1893) and Stevens (1912) – who made their observations well before the era of colleges of education and the rise of progressive education, which some critics (for example, Oldenquist, 1983) blame for contemporary school problems. Hoetker and Ahlbrand (1969) found a 'remarkable stability' in the patterns of instruction described in over a century of reporting, patterns that have been condemned by successive waves of reformers, yet which survived virtually unchanged. These patterns remained so familiar and predictable in US classrooms in the 1980s that they were described as the 'default teaching script' (Cazden, 1988, p.53; Gage and Berliner, 1988, p.539).

TEACHING AS A CULTURAL ACTIVITY

This persistence and stability led many to describe teaching as a 'cultural activity' (Cuban, 1990; Feiman-Nemser and Floden, 1986; Fullan, 1991, 1993; Little and McLaughlin, 1993; Sarason, 1971; Tharp and Gallimore, 1989; Wagner, 1994). This is not good news. Anthropology teaches that cultural change lags behind environmental change (Edgerton, 1992). When an environmental perturbation occurs, the strategy of most individuals and groups is to adapt cautiously, through small experiments on the margins of cultural practice. Activities are modified just enough to make things work – humans are *satisficers* rather than *maximizers* to use Herbert Simon's terms (Simon, 1957), and are generally happy with *just-good-enough* to get by (Edgerton, 1992). Daily routines are compromises between what is *possible* and what is desirable. Little wonder people prefer what they believe to be the most workable arrangements when change involves re-negotiating many hard-won solutions to competing pressures.

Over time, cultural activities and routines are taken for granted and become embodied in beliefs about what is right and proper. This redundancy is the basis of normative behaviours. If 'everyone does the same things' the sources of alternatives are limited.

OBSERVING CLASSROOM PRACTICE
The TIMMS Video Study

One of the major barriers to changing teaching is the narrow range of instructional practices that teachers observe as students. This point was underlined by the Third International Mathematics and Science Study (TIMSS) Video Study, which dramatically illustrated why it is so hard to introduce new teaching practices (Stigler and Hiebert, 1999). As part of TIMMS, the research team conducted a video survey of nationally representative samples in three countries (Germany, Japan, and the US). A video survey is like the more familiar variety, except random samples of lesson are videotaped in numbers sufficient to conduct statistical as well as qualitative analyses. In the TIMSS Video Study, eighth-grade mathematics lessons (for 13 and 14 year olds) were taped during regularly scheduled class periods over the course of a single school term.

After months of watching and analysing lesson videos, the TIMSS team concluded that each nation had a distinctive cultural script for teaching (Stigler and Hiebert, 1999). Although this conclusion was no surprise, the TIMSS video data put in sharp relief a very practical problem. The vivid images captured in the videos made clear how hard it will be to introduce practices aligned to the new curriculum standards: how will teachers ever be able to envisage and implement alternative practices if they seldom see any? *Seeing* that something can be completely different is one of the most effective ways of opening eyes to the ubiquity of cultural practices and creating the circumstances for change.

OBSERVATIONAL LEARNING AS PART OF THE KNOWLEDGE BASE

A general principle of behaviour change theory is that acquisition of complex competencies depends on opportunities for observational learning (Bandura, 1977). To find models, teachers turn to nearby colleagues, or to memories of their own teachers, reinforcing the normative practices that have proven so resistant to change.

Providing teachers with images of alternative practice is more than a question of sending out videotapes. Where will the images of alternative practices be found if so few use them? How can they be aligned to diverse local, regional and national curriculum standards? How will videos of teaching practice be validated as appropriate and effective? Who decides?

Powerful images of alternatives will make a difference only if they are part of a professional knowledge base for teaching. And that is something the US has never developed. Working in relative isolation, individual teachers gradually gain experience and learn what works well in their own classrooms. But their knowledge is shared in only a haphazard manner. As much as they might benefit from the knowledge of their veteran colleagues, most teachers cannot access it and must start over, creating this knowledge anew.

Late in his career, Dewey noted that one of the saddest things about American education is that:

> *...the successes of [excellent teachers] tend to be born and die with them: beneficial consequences extend only to those pupils who have personal contact with the gifted teachers. No one can measure the waste and loss that have come from the fact that the contributions of such men and women in the past have been thus confined.*
>
> *(Dewey, 1929, p.10, with thanks to James Hiebert for this quotation)*

To swim against the tide of culture, and close the teaching gap, will require a rich, broad and validated professional knowledge base that includes vivid images of alternative practices and an environment that both encourages and supports continual improvement of teaching practice.

Designing a professional knowledge base for teaching

We recently attempted to define the characteristics of a professional knowledge base for teaching, how it can be developed, and how the work of practitioners and researchers might contribute (Hiebert, Gallimore and Stigler, 2002). Six design features for a professional knowledge base for teaching were identified. What follows is adapted from our joint efforts.

1. KNOWLEDGE LINKED WITH PRACTICE

Knowledge for teaching is useful when it is developed in response to specific problems of practice. Such knowledge can be applied directly, without translation, but only to a restricted number of situations. It is linked with practice by being grounded in the context in which teachers work and aligned to the content that they are required to teach. The processes that yield knowledge of this sort are collaborative and involve teachers in various forms of joint activities including:

- differentiating problems and developing a shared language for describing them;
- analysing classroom practice in the light of differentiated problems;
- envisaging alternative solutions;
- recursively testing alternatives in the classroom, reflecting on their effects and refining and re-teaching until they are satisfied with the consequences.

2. KNOWLEDGE THAT IS DETAILED, CONCRETE AND SPECIFIC

Knowledge linked with practice is detailed, concrete, and specific. Although the knowledge might apply more generally, it is more often directly related to particular lessons. This differs from the typically propositional knowledge of researchers, which is 'all things equal' and intended to apply to many problems and contexts. Propositional research knowledge can contribute, but it must be processed through multiple observations and replications into practitioner knowledge suited to a specific context, because in each case all things are *not* equal (Goldenberg and Gallimore, 1991).

28

3. KNOWLEDGE THAT IS INTEGRATED

Researchers have identified many kinds of teacher knowledge: for example, content knowledge, pedagogical knowledge and pedagogical content knowledge (Shulman, 1986; Munby, Russell and Martin, 2001). Other kinds of knowledge have been suggested, for example, *the knowledge of students* – what they know and how they learn – that accomplished teachers use to make content comprehensible to learners (Ma, 1999). All the different types of knowledge are intertwined, organised not according to *type* but rather to the *problem* that the knowledge is intended to address. Although it might be possible to identify 'content' as a teacher's knowledge deficiency, or knowledge of what students think on first exposure to a text or problem, it is not helpful to do so if the goal is to improve the teaching of something particular. Knowledge types traditionally separated by investigative analysis must be tightly integrated in order to teach a particular lesson more effectively. This knowledge is linked with practice, and integrated and organised around problems of practice.

To summarise, these first three design features describe the knowledge millions of teachers generate every day. They represent exactly the kinds of knowledge of teaching that teachers both need and want from a professional database. We argue elsewhere that, ultimately, such everyday practitioner knowledge *can* be the principal source of a professional knowledge base for teaching (Hiebert, Gallimore and Stigler, 2002). This pathway, already explored by others (for example, Hargreaves, 1998; for a review see Munby, Russell and Martin, 2001), can be viewed sceptically because practitioners' knowledge is highly personal and, under current conditions, lacks the public vetting of researchers' knowledge. However, its origins in practice provide for the first three of the six features that a professional knowledge base for teaching must include. The other three qualities, described below, transform *practitioner* knowledge into *professional* knowledge (Hiebert *et al.*, 2002).

4. PROFESSIONAL KNOWLEDGE MUST BE PUBLIC

For knowledge, practitioner-generated or otherwise, to become professional knowledge, it must be made public and be represented in such a way that it can be communicated to other members of the profession. Professional knowledge must be created with the intent of public examination, with the goal of making it shareable among teachers, open for discussion, verification, refutation, modification or improvement. Collaborations are essential because they force participants to make their knowledge public and understood by peers during its creation.

5. PROFESSIONAL KNOWLEDGE REQUIRES A MECHANISM FOR VERIFICATION AND IMPROVEMENT

To be professional, knowledge must be accurate, verifiable and continually improving. Teachers working together or with their students might generate knowledge that turns out, in the end, to undermine – rather than improve – teaching effectiveness. Local knowledge is immediate and concrete, but almost always incomplete; sometimes it is blind and insular, or even seriously wrong (Goldenberg and Gallimore, 1991).

To ensure improvement, the insularity of local contexts must be surmounted. One way to assure improvement is the mechanism of multiple observations and replications, which makes it possible over time to secure trustworthy knowledge. Practices must be tried, observed and evaluated in many contexts and the results accumulated and shared over time and location. These are the methods individual teachers have always used to learn to teach – by observing their own practice and later revising it, according to students' feedback and progress.

An analogy can be used here to make the point. Driving through farming land in the US, it is common to see farmers' fields identified as test sites for a grain crop strain. As part of the US agricultural extension system, each year's results are fed into a database, reviewed, indexed and made available to farmers hoping to improve their crops. Many such tests have been conducted every year during the past century. The consequences have been a boon to the American people and economy.

6. PROFESSIONAL KNOWLEDGE MUST BE STORABLE AND SHAREABLE

Even public knowledge is gradually lost if there is no means of accumulating and sharing it across space and time. Practitioner knowledge exists at a particular time and in a specific place. Its life may be extended briefly if shared locally with a small number of colleagues, but this is not sufficient to create a professional knowledge base. Teachers must have a means of storing knowledge in a form that it can be accessed and used by others if it is to take on a life of its own.

Traditionally, teachers wishing to record their knowledge for others have used the most common medium: words on paper. Written records preserve ideas and allow them to be accessed by others. They can be handed across time and space. But the challenge of improving teaching leaves no reason to be optimistic that these conventional means will be sufficient. Talking and writing about teaching is never going to be enough to change the culturally-reinforced practices that were seen again and again in the TIMSS Video Studies (Stigler and Hiebert, 1999; Stigler, Gallimore and Hiebert, 2000) and in dozens of studies since the 1890s. Powerful images of alternatives – and many of them – are required if significant changes are to be achieved. If all teachers ever observe are taken-for-granted cultural teaching scripts, how can we ever hope to improve teaching? The scope of the problem can be represented with a second agricultural analogy:

> *[In the 1800s] it had taken…Coke of Norfolk, sixteen years to persuade his tenants to follow his example and [abandon broadcast planting in favour of the row-culture method], the use of which, he estimated, spread at the rate of only a mile a year. [This despite evidence that row-culture produced twice the yield.]*
>
> *(Bovill, 1962, pp.29–30)*

If opportunities to see alternatives are dependant on teachers occasionally peering into the room next door, changing practices to match new standards will also fall victim to a 'mile a year' rule. If the process takes too long, standards, assessments and other promising reforms may see their political base evaporate. We therefore need to develop a professional knowledge base for teaching that provides teachers with easy access to many alternatives outside their own culturally-constrained practices.

Internet-based technologies are a possibility: this potential was recognised in a National Commission chaired by former US Senator and astronaut John Glenn. To improve the quality of mathematics and science teaching for children aged between five and 16 years (grades K to 12), the Commission urged that:

> ... *a dedicated Internet Portal must be available to teachers so they can make use of and contribute to an ever-expanding knowledge base.*
> *(National Commission on Mathematics and Science Teaching for the 21st Century, 2001)*

Once access and bandwidth issues are resolved, internet and multimedia technologies can potentially make a vast store of knowledge widely and easily accessible to teachers. Because it is now possible to store video and related data that can be accessed over the internet, teachers faced with teaching new topics and lessons could have immediate access to the best ideas accompanied by vivid examples of alternative practices. The content of the knowledge base will have been sifted, evaluated and verified, yielding the standard practices that distinguish the profession (Yinger, 1999).

However, the Glenn Commission sketched only broad goals for an internet approach. The immediate challenge is to consider the design of a technology solution, and by what standards to evaluate it. In the remainder of this chapter, we sketch some design ideas and hypotheses for what we believe an internet solution should include.

A design and some hypotheses for a technology-enabled professional knowledge base

To accumulate a professional knowledge base that is public, shareable and verifiable, we propose that three design components are necessary: digital libraries, user and author interfaces and real and virtual communities. Schematic representations of the system are presented in Figures 3.1 and 3.2 (page 32).

Although technology is attractive as a solution, what the Glenn Commission and many others envisage has not yet been built or tested. Therefore the following should be read as hypotheses rather than prescriptions.

1. HYPOTHESES ABOUT INTERNET-ACCESSED DIGITAL LIBRARIES

To serve the many purposes intended, we hypothesise that progress is more likely to be achieved if many libraries are built, suited to different needs, ranging from those created by a local school system to national and even international ones. From the outset, digital libraries need to be expandable and accessible over the internet using consumer technologies. Some will be developed by institutes of higher education, public and private, professional and technical organisations and commercial entities (for example, to accompany published material).

All libraries need to be indexed and, in this case, curricula are likely to provide the most natural indexing framework for many of these new kinds of libraries. Where teachers share the same curriculum and are expected to teach the same topics, professional knowledge can be indexed with the curriculum.

Lessons may be a practical way to organise and provide access to digital libraries to support improvement of teaching for a number of reasons. Lessons are:

- units of analysis that allow teachers to simplify teaching for study while retaining its essential character;
- contexts within which students' learning are woven together – goals for students' learning, attention to students' thinking, analyses of curriculum and pedagogy, and so on;

- units small enough to enable the complexity of teaching to be reduced to a manageable size.

Figure 3.1: *A schematic representation of the authoring system for Knowledge Base*

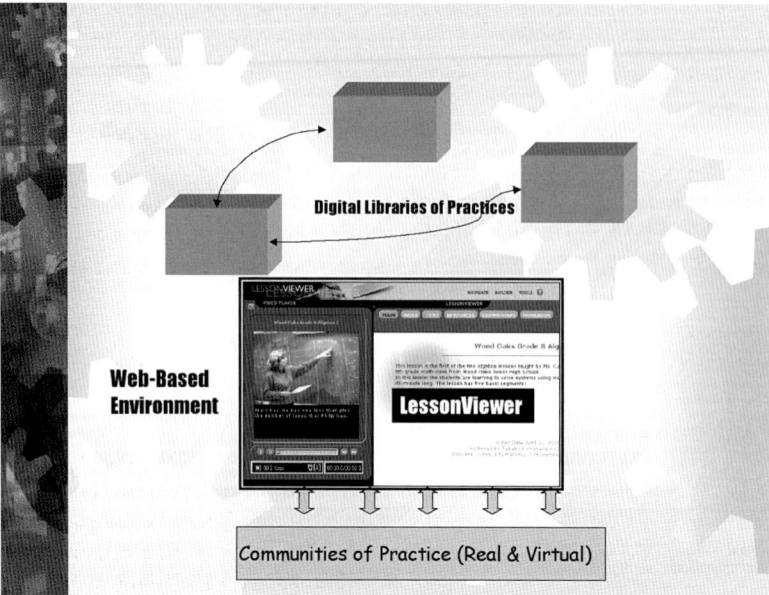

Figure 3.2: *A schematic representation of the web-based environment for Knowledge Base*

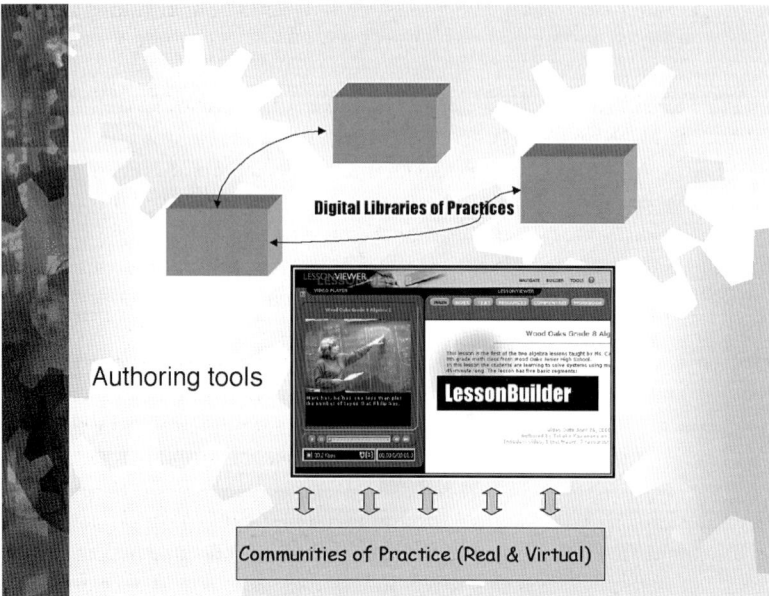

Digital libraries are likely to have more impact if they are built around vivid *images* of practice, rather than *words*. Teaching is complex and hard to capture; words may be interpreted in a variety of ways and much energy in education goes to debating the merits of different practices. The TIMSS Video Study discovered what many already knew: that the words used to talk about teaching often refer to quite different things; what one person means by 'problem solving', for example, is markedly different from what another means (Stigler and Hiebert, 1999).

Learning can be facilitated if the same ideas and concepts are exemplified in a variety of different contexts and using a range of styles. For this reason, we propose that digital libraries include a *large* collection of lesson videos – not just a small collection, and not just lessons taught by charismatic 'star' teachers, whom many admire and few can emulate. Digital libraries that are well-equipped in this way should help teachers envisage a wider range of teaching practices by allowing examination of numerous examples of practice. There is no single way to teach: good results can be obtained with a variety of methods and styles. Just as no good library stocks only a few genres, so too must a digital library of professional knowledge offer plenty of variety and contrast.

The videos in the libraries ought to include plenty of *whole* lessons, or even units of multiple lessons. Limited clips have limited credibility and impact, because the complexities of teaching have been edited out. The theory behind short clips is that teachers should imitate a demonstration and that teaching is a bundle of general pedagogical strategies; the theory that we advocate is that teachers should slow down teaching to analyse it and develop their own professional judgement.

Lesson videos should be surrounded with, and linked to, rich case materials. These should include curriculum standards, lesson plans, images of student work, assessment ideas and examples, commentaries by teachers and researchers and other resources. Images are powerful, but they need to be set in context to support teacher learning.

2. HYPOTHESES ABOUT USER AND AUTHOR INTERFACES
User interface
To help improve teaching, user interfaces that provide access to digital libraries must support *active learning* as well as easy access. Watching lesson videos can be like watching television: you may be entertained, but you won't necessarily learn much.

Teachers, alone and in groups, need an interface so that they can navigate and interact with the lessons and associated resources, enabling them actively to study and learn. The interface should link specific practices in lesson videos to all the resources in the library that are relevant to a given lesson: for example, the previously listed curriculum standards, lesson plans, images of student work, assessment ideas and examples, commentaries by teachers and researchers, and other resources.

The user interface should be designed to enhance teachers' command of the *subject matter* as well as the analysis of *pedagogy*. One way is to provide expert commentaries on lesson content, which are linked to specific parts of the lesson and to supplementary materials and resources. The system should provide for attaching to each lesson links to more information about content, or copies of relevant curriculum and instructional materials. Samples of student work should be attached to the lesson videos so that misunderstandings and errors can be part of the analysis of a lesson. The user interface should provide a way for teachers to communicate with colleagues and expert educators about what they see in lessons, via forums and other means.

Author interface

To stock the libraries with teachers' work, the technology must make authoring of cases widely available and easy to learn. The key to a professional knowledge base is that there is not only wide access, but wide participation in its construction and, as the next section argues, in its review, improvement, and validation. The authoring interface must be inexpensive and easy to use to ensure the full participation of instructional leaders in many kinds of organisations.

It should be possible for authors to design activities for teachers to maximise their learning from study of the lesson videos and associated resources. For example, authors should be able to ask teachers to review their materials. Once they grasp the content, teachers should be able to review a video and mark places in the lesson where they observe particular points. This and similar functions will be needed to transform the digital libraries from a source that teachers are to *imitate* into one that they *study* and use to deepen their understanding and professional judgement.

3. HYPOTHESES ABOUT REAL AND VIRTUAL COMMUNITIES

It is easy enough to imagine communities of users for digital libraries and friendly interfaces. However, the long-term value of professional knowledge, enabled by technology and amplified by videos, depends on the *quality* of what is in the digital libraries: maintaining that quality will be a major challenge. However, the technology envisaged here can both be the means of making professional knowledge available and engaging wide participation in verifying its quality.

The digital libraries we envisage face a major challenge. On the one hand, we want to avoid censorship and ideological purism, on the other we want digital libraries to be repositories of professional knowledge that meet some standard criteria. To realise this, professional organisations and education authorities must work out reviewing procedures. Even at a local level this can be a daunting challenge, and will continue to be so as education struggles to develop a consensus on what constitutes 'standard practice'.

One solution rests within the technology itself. To achieve consensus on what is standard practice, a professional group needs to anchor discussions in practice, not in words about teaching. If the technology were available, it could surely make observation-based deliberations more likely, and that would be a good thing. There is evidence to suggest that when teachers and educators ground discussions of thorny controversies by referring to practice captured in videos, they become more productive and less rhetorical (Saunders and Goldenberg, 1996).

A national example of knowledge production and verification

One model that may offer some ideas for creating communities for the production and validation of professional knowledge is the Japanese system for professional development. Many Japanese elementary school teachers participate, throughout their careers, in a continuing in-service training programme built around the Lesson Study group (Fernandez *et al.*, in press; Lewis and Tsuchida, 1997, 1998; Shimahara, 1998; Shimahara and Sakai, 1995; Takemura and Shimizu, 1993; Yoshida, 1999). Small groups of teachers meet regularly, once a week for several hours, to collaboratively plan, implement, evaluate and revise lessons. The process begins within the Lesson Study group, moves outward to include all teachers in the school, and expands to include teachers in other schools and districts as they review the materials. The knowledge gained from the year-long experience is also represented and stored in a form useful for their colleagues. Eventually those Lesson Studies that are vetted by external reviewers are published in practitioner journals for use by other teachers.

Linking teaching practices to student outcomes

The system sketched may help achieve that most elusive of goals: linking specific teaching practices to student outcomes. Digital libraries of practice give researchers and practitioners in diverse test sites access to the same visual definitions of practice. Such access can support clinical trials in many contexts, thereby enabling robust evaluation of practices through repeated observation and replication. Multiple sites might submit for review video examples of their replication efforts, offering a 'back translation' review of how well the intended changes were actually captured and implemented. Common assessment of student learning associated with practices being evaluated could also be supported by online digital libraries. This offers hope of gradually reaching a consensus on what practices are associated with different levels and kinds of student learning.

Conclusion

Will a professional knowledge base for teaching emerge from technological opportunity? Or will this, like so many promises of technology, prove to be a disappointment? It is too soon to be certain. However, after half a century of trying to disseminate research knowledge in conventional and 'comfortable' ways, it is surely time to entertain other avenues to improve teaching.

Early experience in our laboratory is promising (see www.lessonlab.com/software). Several thousand teachers in three dozen different projects are using a software platform inspired by the TIMSS Video Studies and research on professional development. Some are participating in the building of digital libraries and others are borrowing from those developed elsewhere. The TIMSS-R Video Study released in 2002 a public-use library of eighth-grade mathematics and science lessons (designed for 13 to 14 year olds). Some publishers are providing small libraries of demonstration lessons to accompany their textbooks. Local school systems are using locally-built lesson libraries to implement standards-based instruction, support in-service training programmes and induct new teachers into the profession. A few institutes of higher education are building video cases into online courses to augment traditional programmes.

The stream of activity is small at present, and many major problems have yet to be solved. Among the most challenging is the development of a consensus on what should be available in the library, and who decides what is standard practice.

Amazing technologies and digital libraries will not be enough to close the teaching gap. Like books in libraries, a professional knowledge base of teaching will do no good unless its contents are checked, watched, studied, discussed, improved, augmented and the ideas woven into existing knowledge and practice. To make effective use of a professional knowledge base, teachers need to be part of a professional development programme that is long term and coherently integrated into ongoing reform activities in their school and district.

For digital libraries to function as envisaged, educators will need to find a way to agree on what constitutes standard practice. Standard practices, according to Al Shanker, the American union leader, distinguish a profession (Shanker, 1995); the establishment of such practices is their proper aim, provided that there is also a means of improving them over time. In medicine, failure to follow the standard practice is *malpractice*. The new technologies that are now available can help make teaching a profession defined by its knowledge base, which will allow it to improve its practices over time (Yinger, 1999). Over the past 100 years, medicine has changed greatly – not because smarter people became doctors, but because medicine found a way to accumulate and share knowledge and to update and improve it over time. If we begin now, and take advantage of the new technologies, perhaps the same will be true of teaching within the next generation.

----

4 'When ready' testing

Martin Ripley and Sue Walton
Qualifications and Curriculum Authority (QCA), London, UK

Introduction

IN THE UK THERE ARE A NUMBER OF TEST MODELS in existence, most involving a test being taken at the *end* of a course or unit of study. In the majority of cases, the test takes place on a prescribed date and at a time fixed by an awarding body or test provider. However with the growing interest in, and expectation of, 'anytime and anywhere' learning, particularly in the context of computer-delivered courses, a corresponding interest in 'when ready' testing has grown.

The UK Government is also showing interest in the idea of more flexibility in testing as part of its raising standards agenda and its desire to ensure that students reach their full potential. For example, in relation to the key stage 3 strategy (aimed at students aged from 11 to 14 years):

> ... *we want to see all pupils stretched so that they achieve their full potential ... We want to see further increases in the extent of setting within subjects, including express sets to enable those who are capable of doing so to advance beyond the levels set for their age and to take key stage 3 tests early.*
>
> *(GB.DfEE, 2001, p.51)*

This was articulated even more clearly in the White Paper *Schools Achieving Success*:

> *We are developing an online ICT test to assess pupils' ability to research, manage and evaluate information. It will pioneer a new, flexible approach to testing so that pupils can take the test as soon as they are ready. Over time, we will seek to build on this approach.*
>
> *(GB.DfES, 2001, p.20)*

The move towards greater flexibility and a focus on individual student needs was also promoted in the Green Paper *14–19: Extending Opportunities, Raising Standards* (GB.DfES, 2002). This paper suggests that a student should be allowed to progress faster or slower according to their ability and also proposes the idea of an individual learning plan.

What is 'when ready' testing?

'When ready' testing is a flexible model for testing that can cover a spectrum of options:

- At one end of the spectrum, flexibility might be achieved by simply increasing the number of fixed dates on which tests are available. For example, instead of *one* set date for a particular test, there might be *four* set dates throughout the year – so if a student misses a date or is 'not ready' they will only have to wait three months until the next possible date.

- At the opposite end of the spectrum is the possibility of a student literally taking a test when they wish to or feel 'ready' – by, for example, logging onto a website at a time to suit them.

- Testing 'when ready' also includes modular testing. Thus, in a situation where a student needs to complete a number of papers or components to meet the full requirements of a test or qualification, those components might be offered on fixed occasions or throughout a course of study. Credit on each component is carried forward until such time as the student has met the requirements for all the components.

A working definition of 'when ready' testing might therefore be 'any test that can be taken at a point in time which matches the learning programme of the student'. The concept also embodies a shift of control over the timing of a test away from administrators to students and teachers and additionally an increase in flexibility.

ISSUES ARISING

Flexibility in testing arrangements raises a number of issues:

- There is a potential tension between the need of an individual student to progress and a teacher's need to manage a whole class. This raises the issue of how much differentiation a teacher can handle in practice.

- The concept of a student being tested when they are ready also sits uncomfortably alongside current regulations for public examinations, which prohibit students from making multiple attempts at, for example, a General Certificate of Secondary Education (GCSE) examination until they pass or achieve a particular grade. There is inconsistency in allowing flexibility as to when a test is taken but not allowing a similar level of flexibility in resitting, particularly bearing in mind the potential for misjudging readiness by either the student or their teacher.

- Monitoring standards over time and for a particular cohort can become problematic if students are taking tests at different times and ages. This raises issues of both comparability and fairness.

- 'When ready' testing has the potential to allow assessments to be used formatively by allowing students to understand their areas of weakness following a test attempt and to make improvements before attempting the test again. This moves the focus of testing away from assessment *of* learning towards assessment *for* learning.

Examples of 'when ready' tests

MODULAR TESTS

Modular testing enables candidates to take a series of test papers throughout a course, rather than having all the assessment at the end. Such tests are 'when ready' in that candidates take them as soon as they are able to: that is, as soon as they have completed a unit of study (although the dates for such tests are usually confined to one or two prescribed dates a year).

A levels and AS levels

Many qualifications use this pattern of assessment. The A levels (both general and vocational) introduced in September 2000 are 'modular'. Traditional A levels had linear forms of assessment, with all examinations taken at the end of the course. Since the early 1990s there has been a move towards increasing modularity within A levels, culminating in 2000 with the introduction of modular assessment in all A level qualifications. Their vocational counterparts – previously known as advanced General National Vocational Qualifications (GNVQs), now known as vocational A levels – have employed a modular approach to assessment since their introduction in the 1990s. Critics of the traditional A level system of assessment pointed to the motivating effect on students of modular assessment. Regular feedback, both to students and their teachers, was felt to be an important factor contributing to greater attainment. Presenting both learning and assessment in more manageable chunks was also felt to support the wider range of learners continuing their studies post-16. Additionally, there was concern that many students dropped out of the course before the end and had nothing to show for their studies. The move towards modular assessment has also, however, had its critics. Concerns have been raised about the potential threat to standards by reducing the amount of terminal assessment and about the manageability – for both students and the institutions they learn in – of increased assessment opportunities.

These concerns were addressed during the development of the new A levels. The A level qualification introduced in 2000 as part of 'Curriculum 2000' is broken down into six assessment units – usually linked directly to six teaching modules (referred to as units). The first three Advanced Subsidiary (AS) units are assessed at a standard appropriate for students halfway through an advanced level course of study and are therefore less demanding than the full Advanced (A) level standard. The remaining three (A2) units are more demanding, and include a synoptic unit that requires students to draw together and apply their understanding across a subject. The demanding synoptic units, along with the remaining A2 units, in combination with the AS units, are designed to maintain the overall level of demand of the full A level qualification.

Two qualifications can be obtained – an AS comprising the first three units and a full A level comprising both the AS and the A2 units. The new system provides students and their institutions with considerable flexibility over when units are assessed. Examination sessions are available in the January and June of each year, with students able to use these sessions as they wish. They have the option of taking exams in some of the modules at particular points in their course or leaving all the exams until the end of their period of study. All assessment units may be resat once. Full qualifications can be resat an unlimited number of times. Students can decide whether or not they wish to 'cash-in' their unit results when they have completed the requisite number of units for the award of a qualification (either AS or the full A level). This system is designed to provide students with maximum flexibility over resitting units.

TESTS OFFERED ON A RANGE OF DATES
Most 'when ready' testing in the UK currently falls into this category, which encompasses both multiple test dates and 'windows' of dates.

Musical instrument examinations
Musical instrument examinations are one example. Here, students follow the syllabus for a particular grade for a particular musical instrument. The largest UK examining body, the Associated Board of the Royal Schools of Music (see www.abrsm.ac.uk) offers three five-week windows of dates (one per school term) with entry having to be made six weeks before the beginning of the window. These exams are pass/fail tests and typically students work their way up through the grades taking each graded exam when they are ready.

Business skills examinations
Examinations in business areas, such as text processing, are another example. There is a long history of this type of exam being 'on demand'. These examinations were originally qualifications for the workplace, with courses typically being taken by students at night school or secretarial college; more recently, they have been offered by FE colleges because of their acceptibility to employers. As with graded music examinations, students start at one level and, having passed the test, then move on to work towards the next level. Availability of dates for testing is very wide. For example, in the current academic year, the Oxford, Cambridge and Royal Society of Arts (OCR) awarding body (see www.ocr.org.uk) is offering 10 windows of two or three weeks in length, with students able to take the test on any of the dates in the window.

Other examples
Other examples of tests offered on a range of dates include:
- the tests of competence in English, mathematics and ICT for trainee teachers (www.canteach.gov.uk) – see also Chapter 7;
- the basic skills tests in literacy and numeracy (for example, www.city-and-guilds.co.uk) – see also Chapter 8;
- the World Class Arena tests in mathematics and problem solving aimed at gifted and talented students at the ages of nine and 13 (www.worldclassarena.org.uk) – see also Chapter 12;
- the theory and practical elements of the UK driving test (www.driving-tests.co.uk).

TESTS OFFERED ON A TOTALLY 'WHEN READY' BASIS: FLEXIBLE AVAILABILITY
National tests in Scotland

The national tests in Scotland for students aged from five to 14 years fall into this category (Scottish Examination Board, 1993; see also www.sqa.org.uk). These tests (in English and mathematics) are used to complement and confirm teachers' ongoing assessments of student progress at primary school (P1 to P6) and the first two years of secondary school (S1 and S2). The Scottish 5–14 curriculum covers six levels of difficulty. When a teacher judges that a student is ready to move from one level to the next, he or she chooses and orders an appropriate test from a national bank of test units and then administers the test. Students are therefore tested when they are ready to move from one level to the next and not at any particular age or stage as is the case, for example, with national testing in England. The tests can be taken at any time in the school year and are carried out as part of normal classroom activity.

Other examples

Most other examples of totally 'when ready' tests occur in lower stakes situations. One example is the tests for schools produced by GOAL (www.goalplc.co.uk), which can be taken at any time of the schools' choosing. Many websites offering revision help also have tests that students can attempt at any time – for example, BBC Bitesize (www.bbc.co.uk/schools) and Sam Learning (www.samlearning.com). Standardised tests such as the *Cognitive Abilities Test (CAT)* (Thorndike *et al.*, 2001), used principally in the UK for predicting GCSE grades, may also be used at any time.

Online training

Online training courses also usually have tests that students can take to fit in with their 'anytime anywhere' learning. Courses produced by SmartForce (www.smartforce.com) are one example here. SmartForce follow a four-pronged approach: learners begin with the *instruction* mode and then move into a *practice* mode, followed by a *collaboration* mode, where they can reinforce their learning. In the *assessment* mode, they take tests to check how much they have learned, where they still have weaknesses and whether or not their learning objectives have been met. Like the other modes, the assessment mode is available at any time and is particularly targeted at learners who are undertaking training in their own time and possibly away from the workplace.

National qualifications

'When ready' testing has not, to date, been a feature of mainstream national qualifications such as GCSE and A level. The quality assurance procedures (codified through criteria and Codes of Practice) associated with these qualifications do not prevent a move towards 'when ready' testing, but would need to be carefully reviewed to ensure compatability between assessment practice and the need to maintain examination standards within the system.

Models for 'when ready' testing and some examples are summarised in Table 4.1 on page 42.

Table 4.1: *Models for 'when ready' testing*

	VARIABLE CONTENT	VARIABLE AND FIXED CONTENT	FIXED CONTENT
Modular/ fixed dates	• national curriculum tests (ages 11 and 14 years: key stages 2 and 3); • AS/A2 examinations.		
Range of dates/ test windows	• basic skills tests; • trainee teacher tests; • World Class Arena tests; • text processing tests; • national curriculum tests (age 7 years: key stage 1).	• musical instrument examinations; • driving tests.	
Flexible availability			• GOAL tests; • BBC Bitesize tests; • SmartForce tests; • standardised tests, e.g. *Cognitive Abilities Test*; • Scotland 5–14 national tests.

'When ready' for what?

The concept of testing 'when ready' also raises the question of *what* it is the student is actually 'ready' for. Tests can be used for different purposes:

- to *confirm that a standard has been reached* – tests used for this purpose are normally pass/fail tests and are usually taken when learners (or their teachers) think that they are ready to pass because they have acquired all the necessary skills and knowledge;
- to *record progress and/or achievement* – tests can be used to record achievement formally, for example at the end of a course or module ('high stakes') or they can be used to record progress informally, for example, a test set by a teacher at the end of a unit of work (lower stakes);
- to *aid future learning* – tests can also be used diagnostically to check strengths and weaknesses and to inform next steps.

Some tests serve more than one of these purposes.

In the case of tests offered on a range of dates, the tests are principally being used to confirm that a standard has been reached. These tests all embody the notion of passing or failing and all the examples quoted assume that the student is ready to take a test because they expect to pass (normally in a high stakes situation). So in these kinds of tests, 'readiness' actually means ready to jump through the hoops needed to pass – success being the expectation. The Scottish 5–14 tests also fit this pattern, although as results are only available to the student, school and parents the stakes are relatively low.

Modular tests and tests such as the national curriculum tests in England, are principally concerned with recording achievement, although in doing so they also confirm a standard. Tests in this category often occur at educational 'milestones' – for example, the transfer from one stage of schooling or education to the next.

The other examples of tests given above are different and are more to do with checking learning so, for example, students using BBC Bitesize revise a topic and then do a test to see if they can remember what they have revised. They get instant feedback on their success in the form of both a score and comments about weaknesses. Here there is no sense of pass and fail. This is typical of this category of 'when ready' test and suggests that such tests are concerned more with formative assessment – that is, helping the student identify strengths and weaknesses so that they can improve. There is usually no limit to the number of times students can attempt these tests so they can resit until they feel they have achieved the level they wish.

The pros and cons of 'when ready' testing

BENEFITS
Testing when ready offers a number of potential benefits.

For students
For students the benefits are:

• Being able to *take a test when they are ready to*, rather than having to wait (or take the test too early). This could allow students to progress at their own pace, meaning that, for example, they might be able to progress more quickly.

• The possibility of such *assessments being used more formatively*, to input more into learning than is normally the case with tests. The low stakes examples cited above already provide this kind of support by outlining where students have made mistakes and often giving an explanation of why an answer is not correct. Online courses often also suggest the remedial action needed such as revising a particular topic or reading a specific unit. In a high stakes test environment this might still be possible particularly if resits were allowed and the test was online. A student could, for example, attempt a national curriculum test early in a key stage to identify what level they are at as well as their strengths and weaknesses. After spending time addressing their weaknesses they could then resit the test. This could work with both pass/fail situations and situations where a level is awarded.

• Where tests are computer based there might be an increased opportunity to design *tests tailored to the needs of the individual student*. Such 'adaptive' tests offer new models of testing. For example, in a pass/fail environment the test could simply end when the student has reached the 'pass' threshold. In a test environment where students are being assessed against a range of levels (as with national curriculum assessments) students could have a common entry point to a test but, depending on how they respond, would be taken to different levels by the computer. Here the test might continue until a student has reached a particular level but has been unable to demonstrate sufficient evidence of achievement at the level above. In both these situations, tests would take varying lengths of time to complete depending on

43

student performance. For many students, test timings could be reduced: time would not be wasted answering inappropriate or unnecessary questions because a required standard has already been demonstrated.

For schools and administrators

For schools and administrators the benefits are:

- The potential of *greater organisational flexibility* for students and schools by enabling them to organise test occasions to suit their own schedule and requirements. This might lead to lower resource requirements. For example, if the test is computer based, less hardware might be needed as it could be assumed that students would be taking tests at different times. Similarly, fewer markers might also be needed because the period in which scripts need to be marked would be spread over a longer time period, or marking might be automated if the test were computer based.

- *Lower-cost tests*, since – depending on the context and stakes – it might be acceptable to have only one test or a bank of tests, rather than a new test for each test session. Spreading the testing window may also reduce costs such as marking. However, please note that – to date – there are no known examples of computer-based test systems costing less than tests that were previously paper based.

DISADVANTAGES

As well as possible advantages of this kind of testing there are also a number of potential disadvantages.

For students

Disadvantages for students include:

- A possible *lowering of test results* in general. If students take a test as soon as they are ready, they might be expected to obtain a lower grade or score than if they had taken the test later.

- When ready testing may work *better for some subject areas than for others*, for example, skills-based subjects and subjects that lend themselves to being broken up into limited blocks of knowledge that can be assessed in isolation.

- There may be *increased pressure for students* if there is no set timetable for testing. Students may feel that as soon as they have mastered a particular level or set of skills, they will be tested. This could be seen as a 'punishment for progressing', and certainly not as a reward.

For schools and administrators

Disadvantages for schools and administrators include:

- Possible *accentuation of security issues* if the tests are high stakes. For example, if students take the same test over a period of time, rather than on the same date, it will be difficult to prevent students taking the test later in the cycle from finding out what the test items are. This may not be an issue if the assessment is testing skills, but it could undermine the validity of the test result where knowledge and understanding are being assessed. The security issue could be reduced if there were a bank of tests as the student would not be able to predict which test they would be presented with. Security issues might also be reduced if adaptive test models were used, as each student would have their own customised test and therefore potential cheating would be made difficult.

- *Possible dumbing down of test results*, with students obtaining a lower grade or score than might have been the case if they had taken the test later. This has implications for measuring the value added by a school.

- A *potentially increased organisational and administrative burden* on schools. The model puts the onus of date and time selection onto the school, and adding extra test dates could cause problems both for timetabling and availability of test facilities – for example, it may be difficult to find an invigilator who is available at the appropriate time.

For awarding bodies and the Government
Disadvantages for awarding bodies and the Government include:

- *An increased volume of test materials* may be needed if there is a requirement for a different test for each test date.

- *Maintaining consistency in standards and test conditions may be more difficult* as more tests are being taken at a variety of times.

Using ICT in the Administration of Tests

Overview

Chris Collins

Independent management consultant, London, UK

Martyn Roads

Independent education and assessment consultant, Maidstone, UK

Part II identifies the nature of the benefits, risks and issues that can be associated with increased ICT deployment. Many of the issues and opportunities discussed are based on direct experience gained during ICT-based developments. In examining the issues, further evidence is provided that many of the issues arising are not unique to individual projects, and that they could perhaps be better addressed within an industry-wide focus.

In Chapter 5, we show the place of ICT in the assessment process by first describing the generic development and implementation of assessment and the different stages involved. Based on the work of a QCA study (Collins and Roads, 2002), the chapter examines opportunities for further ICT deployment and the potential benefits at each stage. The possible drivers for future technological changes are identified; potential barriers that may inhibit the speed or scope of on-screen assessment are also explored. The chapter finishes with an analysis of the often-quoted benefits of ICT in assessment by providing an insight into the circumstances in which the benefits might be realised, and by identifying their key beneficiary – candidate or test provider?

Chapter 6, by Alastair Walker, describes the approach taken by the Northern Ireland Council for the Curriculum, Examinations and Assessment (CCEA) to apply new technology to assessment and examinations. Two projects are described: the Paperless Examinations Project (PEP), which focuses on 'high stakes' summative public examinations, and the Assessment for Learning Project, which addresses formative assessment in the classroom. On the PEP project, undertaken with Edexcel, GCSE science and geography for 16 year olds were chosen for the first trials, as these subjects contain questions where innovative use can be made of ICT delivery and where marking can be automated. The project identifies that ICT can assist in reducing demand for markers but brings to our attention a number of ergonomic, administrative and logistics issues. The aims of the Assessment for Learning Project are to provide computer-based methods of classroom assessment that facilitate good quality feedback, and record-keeping facilities for subsequent compiling of summative reports. Although dealing with different areas of testing, both CCEA projects identify the potential of ICT for teaching and learning, and the impact this may have on teacher training and development. If ICT is to help realise significant educational benefits, the curriculum, learning and assessment processes need to be transformed as one.

In Chapter 7, Angela Walsh provides another example of ICT being introduced to deliver high stakes testing. In July 1999, the Teacher Training Agency commenced the development and implementation of the Qualified Teacher Status Skills Tests: computed-based literacy, numeracy and ICT tests, embodying standards to be attained by all trainee teachers. Against a set of operational requirements, the first computerised tests were introduced in 2001. The chapter provides examples of on-screen test material and describes the limitations and benefits of the delivery systems. For example, ensuring the technical stability of tests came to be regarded as a vital prerequisite in the success of their delivery.

Chapter 8, by Michael Kingdon, outlines experiences from the QCA-led pilot into the provision of ICT-based basic and key skills tests. The chapter describes how the project was set up and the different test delivery models that might be operated by awarding bodies depending on the needs of centres. The project suggests that there is likely to be a 'mixed economy' of delivery approaches, and that in time we will need to give more attention to the management of markers, on-demand delivery, item and test comparability and changes to regulation and compliance processes.

The opportunities for ICT in assessment

Chris Collins
Independent management consultant, London, UK

Martin Ripley
Qualifications and Curriculum Authority (QCA), London, UK

Martyn Roads
Independent education and assessment consultant, Maidstone, UK

Introduction

SOME COMMENTATORS AND EXPERTS in the area of assessment make profound claims for the potential of technology in application to assessment processes (for example, Bennett and Persky, 2002). They argue that radical change to our assessment systems will occur as a result of this inevitable progression. In fact there are already in the UK a number of assessment systems that have extended our understanding of the ways in which technology can be used to rethink the assessment process. The Teacher Training Agency (TTA) Skills Tests (see pages 77 to 90), the QCA World Class Tests and the Theory Driving Test are significant and high-profile assessments that use technology in different ways. Some developments are designed to make use of technology in the administrative aspects of assessment systems whilst others use scanning technology in marking students' work. This chapter describes the opportunities offered by these developments and explores clues about the possible nature of assessment in the future.

The chapter also looks at the nature of the main assessment processes used in England, covering the testing of students aged between five and 14 years (key stages 1 to 3) and public examinations. It describes the areas within those processes where technology can be, and is being, applied, and looks at the main drivers for change and for greater use of ICT within the assessment processes.

Why use technology in educational assessment?

The size, scale and importance of the assessment industry in the UK are already leading us to look at the ways in which technology can improve processes and reduce risk. The numbers involved in that industry are huge. The key skills project run by QCA (see pages 91 to 101) is planning to include 40,000 hours of pre-testing material each year. The key stage 2 and 3 tests in England (designed for 11 and 14 year olds) involve 1,200,000 students each completing tests in three subjects, and each subject consisting of either two or three hard-copy papers – this results in 7.2 million test scripts being moved around the country. Approximately 23 million examinations at General Certificate of Secondary Education (GCSE), Advanced Subsidiary (AS) and Advanced (A) level are completed annually. Numerous vocational qualifications are also completed. In addition to this there are many other forms of tests and examinations that fall outside the formal and statutory frameworks that govern examination centres (that is, schools, colleges and training providers).

The timescales are also profoundly concerning. The 7.2 million key stage 2 and 3 test scripts are marked between mid-May and mid-July. This period includes time for postage, checking, auditing and data return. Such is the scale of the data captured through these processes that the Department for Education and Skills (DfES) is unable to prepare final results files for publication purposes until October each year.

These considerations alone provide sufficient justification for the examination of technology and the assessment process provided in this chapter.

Assessment stages

In 2002, QCA undertook a review of the use of ICT in assessment (Collins and Roads, 2002). This review looked at the current and potential ways in which technology might be deployed in different stages of the assessment processes. The description below outlines the distinct stages that feature in most assessment processes – beginning with the identification of the need for a test, and generally ending with the notification of results and certification. Each stage is examined with respect to current and potential ICT deployment.

The 15 stages described have evolved into processes that can occupy a period of up to 34 months – almost three years – from the beginnings of the test development process through to the notification of results. The assessment processes, and their associated timescales, are illustrated in general terms in Figures 5.1 and 5.2 (see pages 53 and 54).

STAGE 1: IDENTIFICATION OF THE NEED TO ASSESS
This stage is not normally considered part of the process of developing the assessment tools or instruments. Rather, it identifies the need for the qualification and develops the qualification specification. It includes decisions on the type of assessment to be used.

Potential for using technology
It is unlikely that technology could have any significant impact on this stage.

STAGE 2: DESIGN OF ASSESSMENT INSTRUMENTS

In Stage 2, the style of assessment instrument (test, examination, coursework) is developed. This includes the test specification and all the other criteria that will enable examiners to prepare and author tests, and will form part of the published qualification specification.

Potential for using technology

It is unlikely that technology could have any significant impact on this stage.

STAGE 3: PREPARATION, AUTHORING AND CALIBRATION

In this stage, the individual test items or examination questions are developed through a process of authoring, editing, reviewing and proofing. This process includes developing the marking scheme. It will usually be undertaken every time an examination is required – often at least twice a year.

Potential for using technology

There is limited ICT use at present, although some private sector companies are developing software to support the authoring process, particularly in the generation of multiple-choice forms of questioning (for example, the QuestionMark software; see www.questionmark.com). More innovative projects, such as the World Class Arena project, are developing systems that support the authoring of more complex and dynamic test items and activities.

STAGE 4: PRE-TESTING

In Stage 4, where the assessment process requires that the pass mark or grade boundaries are determined in advance, or where the items are being placed in an item bank to be used in a number of different papers, items are pre-tested. Pre-testing is also used extensively in England in the development of tests at key stages 1, 2 and 3, in order to refine the item presentation to students. Overall, however, very few tests and examinations used in England are pre-tested.

Potential for using technology

Significant use of technology could be made in pre-testing items but there is little use of technology in this area currently.

STAGE 5: ENTRY/REGISTRATION

In Stage 5, students, schools and examination candidates notify the awarding body, QCA or other body that they intend to sit a particular examination or test; this stage also includes the processes of checking and amending registration and entry details.

Potential for using technology

QCA currently encourages schools to supply students' names for key stage testing electronically. In addition, awarding bodies enable centres to submit entry details electronically. However, this procedure uses old technology, is cumbersome and, although used for 85 per cent of school entries, has not been extended into other testing and assessment activities.

Through the Pupil Level Annual Schools Census (PLASC) project, test administrators are looking for opportunities to obtain pupil and school details to support their own requirements. As the PLASC core database develops, it should provide a more integrated approach to data-sharing, and could even include the requirements of other examinations in addition to key stage 2 and 3 tests.

Of all the assessment stages, Stage 5 offers perhaps the greatest potential to bring very real and useful benefits to examination centres.

STAGE 6: PRINTING AND DISTRIBUTION
Stage 6 covers typesetting and printing the test/examination paper, and distributing it (either by conventional or electronic means) to examination centres.

Potential for using technology
Increasingly, tests are being distributed electronically, although some, on receipt at the centre, are then reproduced in hard copy for delivery of the traditional paper-based test. A few pilot projects, described elsewhere in this book, have begun to look at distributive processes – the World Class Arena project currently distributes paper-based tests in hard copy to schools and test centres, but uses electronic media for on-screen and online tests. Some of the awarding bodies, such as the Institute of the Motor Industry (IMI), have begun to implement electronic distribution processes for key skills and vocational qualifications.

There is clearly significant potential for the use of ICT to distribute tests electronically.

STAGE 7: AUTHENTICATION
Stage 7 describes the process by which the examination centre confirms the identity of the student and the validity of the details relating to the examination being taken.

Potential for using technology
At present, these processes are predominantly paper-based in respect of national curriculum assessment, although awarding bodies and their centres are making greater use of technology. Some use could be made of ICT, although the benefits in terms of time, cost and workload might not be significant.

STAGE 8: PRESENTATION
In this stage, the test or examination paper is delivered to the student or the candidate. For paper-based examinations, this will consist of the setting up of an invigilated examination room. For on-screen delivery, the process will involve loading the assessment software and making ready the candidate's PC environment.

Potential for using technology
Further significant use could be made of ICT to deliver on-screen ICT-based assessment, although recent feedback from pilot projects and initiatives suggests that further work is required to develop suitable standards for test operation in centres. This should address issues such as test environment design, technical reliability, security and confidentiality.

Figure 5.1: *The generic assessment process: Stages 1 to 6*

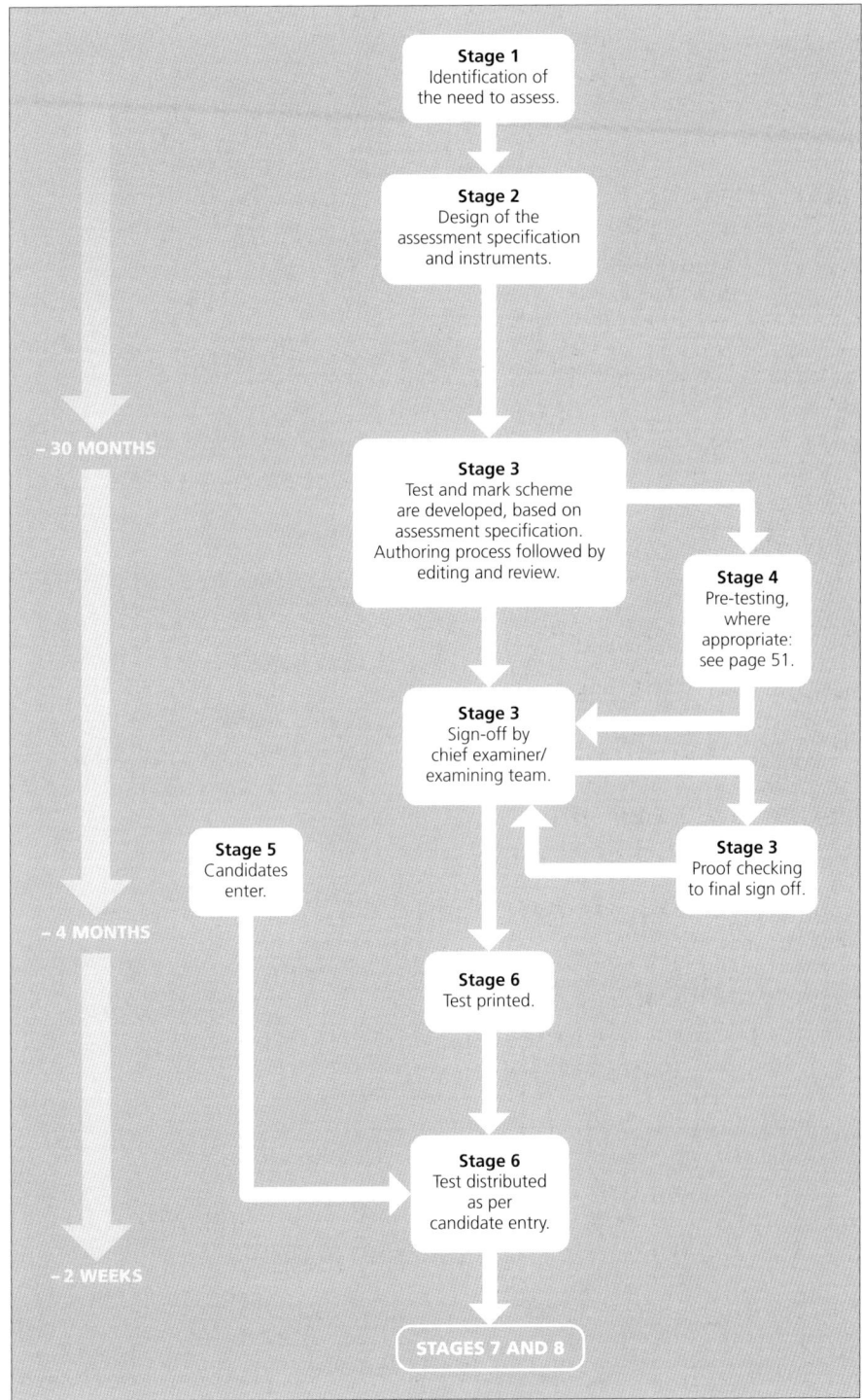

Figure 5.2: *The generic assessment process: Stages 7 to 15*

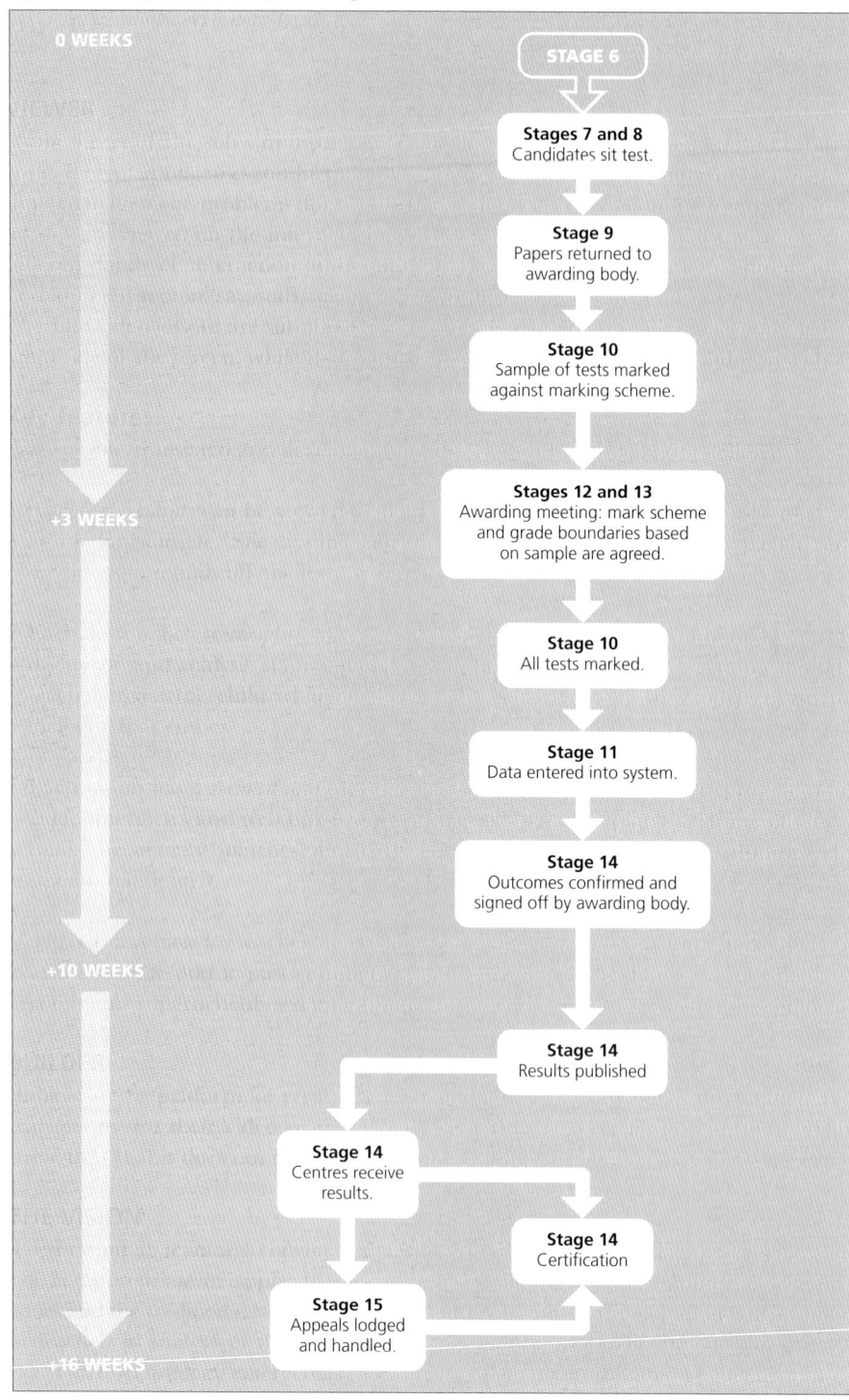

STAGE 9: RESPONSE RETURN

This is the process by which the students and candidates make their responses for subsequent marking. The vast majority of responses are currently both captured and marked on paper. In some other tests and examinations use is made of:

• *optical mark reader sheets (OMR)*: for example, in the key skills tests and adult literacy and numeracy tests levels 1 (foundation) and 2 (intermediate);
• *scanning hard-copy question booklets* or papers for subsequent on-screen marking (for example, QCA has, since 2000, been investigating the effectiveness of scanning for marking purposes);
• *electronic data files*: for example, the World Class Arena project currently offers automatically marked tests on an online basis (see www.worldclassarena.org) as well as capturing students' responses to on-screen tests and presenting these both for automatic marking and for human interrogation.

Potential for using technology

The potential offered by on-screen delivery and the increased ability to analyse the candidate's every response could significantly change the nature of tests in the future. First, however, the reliability of the technology and the automated marking regimes must be further researched and proven.

STAGE 10: MARKING/SCORING

Stage 10 covers the entire marking process for a candidate's responses and concludes by generating the overall results or score.

Potential for using technology

There are some projects that already use technology in the marking process, although this represents limited ICT usage in relation to the overall size of the UK assessment industry. However, the potential efficiency benefits and reductions in the demand for human markers are very significant, and are likely to lead QCA and awarding bodies to look seriously at this benefit potential.

STAGE 11: DATA RETURN

At Stage 11, all the examination and test results, at whatever level of detail, are captured by awarding bodies and by QCA on their examination systems.

Potential for using technology

The UK's main data capture method currently involves double keying the input of results to ensure data quality. Use is currently made of OMR, where assessors record marks awarded to candidates on OMR forms that are then scanned for electronic capture. A principal benefit of on-screen delivery is that results data capture is automatic if the test is marked by computer. This eliminates the time and cost of manual data keying and avoids the possibility of introducing errors into the results. The QCA scanning pilots for the key stage 2 and 3 test scripts have also changed the data return process, in that electronic scripts are presented to assessors for on-screen marking and recording results.

STAGE 12: ANALYSIS

Stage 12 describes the process used to analyse the examination and test data.

Potential for using technology

This process is already well supported by ICT facilities. Consequently, there is less opportunity to realise significant further benefits from ICT, although as other stages in the assessment process become increasingly technology and data rich, more timely and better intelligence from the data analysis process is likely to result.

STAGE 13: AWARDING AND STANDARDISATION

Stage 13 determines the pass mark and/or grade boundaries for the examination, using the statistics provided by the analysis process. This ensures consistency of standards over time and, in some cases, provides the opportunity to eliminate any items that performed poorly in the examination. (The process is not required when items have already been pre-tested extensively to allow a predetermined pass mark to be set, as is the case with the Theory Driving Test.)

Potential for using technology

As ICT is already well used in this process, there is limited opportunity for further deployment.

STAGE 14: RESULTS PUBLISHING AND CERTIFICATION

In this stage, results are published and certificates issued to candidates following the awarding and standardisation process. For fully computerised assessment, this may be an integral part of Stage 10, when scores and results can be given to candidates very soon after they have completed the test. However, there are very few instances in assessment where this form of notification of results is currently a feature. Most large-scale assessments in the UK involve Stage 13, as well as requiring quality assurance of the marking and data capture process before results are returned to centres.

Potential for using technology

There is very significant potential for the use of technology at this stage, particularly when combined with use at Stages 6, 8, 9 and 10.

STAGE 15: APPEALS

This is the final assessment stage, and comprises a process by which schools, colleges and test centres can lodge appeals against results, requesting a review of the results given. There are several sub-stages available for public examinations in the UK with a final appeal to an independent review body.

Potential for using technology

Although there is very little potential for technology to be applied at the appeals stage, it is clear that the nature of the appeal could be significantly altered through changes in Stage 9 (Student and candidate response mode) and Stage 10 (Marking mode). Where hard copy scripts are no longer available for appeals, or where marking has been carried out automatically, the basis for appeals is likely to change.

 As is clear from the descriptions above, some of the most time-consuming parts of the process are those that least lend themselves to the application of technology. For example, the development and authoring of the test is the process that takes the greatest amount of time. There are some projects in the UK that are looking at ways of generating tests automatically: this involves calling up pre-written items from a bank or archive to compile a new test that complies with a test specification. Many of the existing tests used in the UK may not be capable of this form of test generation, although the key skills tests based on multiple-choice questions, currently undergoing a trial with GOAL plc, may be suitable for automatic compilation in the future. Another example is the period between Stage 7 (when the candidates sit the tests) and Stage 11 (data return), where there are opportunities to significantly reduce the timeframe of approximately 10 weeks. By using the generic assessment model, we can better analyse where the potential benefits of deploying technology might be realised and what impact implementation may have on the overall process.

Drivers for technological change

The potential increase in demand for extending the use of ICT in the assessment process in the UK might be stimulated by a number of drivers. Although it is perhaps easier to identify their nature, it is more difficult to predict the speed and direction that an individual driver or technological innovation may take or what their collective impact may be over a 20-year planning horizon. Some of the worldwide impacts of technological changes that have occurred during the last 25 years would have been difficult to foresee in the mid-1970s. What is certain is that technological advances in computing-related areas will continue, some of which will present further opportunities in the area of assessment. The potential drivers that could generate increased demand for ICT assessment are discussed below. Each of these drivers could, in the context of a national strategy, take on greater or lesser significance in shaping the use made of technology.

CENTRAL GOVERNMENT INITIATIVES

The Government's own initiatives have been increasingly geared towards positioning the UK as a knowledge-based economy. These initiatives can be divided into 'How government delivers using ICT' and 'How we learn using ICT'. The former includes examples such as the *Modernising Government* agenda (GB.Cabinet Office, 1999), government websites for disseminating information about services and events, and the Inland Revenue's web facilities for self-assessment. The latter includes initiatives that are aimed at raising individuals' skill levels through lifelong learning opportunities and vocational training, such as e-Learning, the University for Industry, the LearnDirect centres and the National Grid for Learning. In addition, the ways in which particular projects are used could have a significant impact in terms of defining solutions and standards: for example, the World Class Arena project, the key stage 3 ICT tests project, the key skills tests and adult literacy and numeracy tests.

CHANGES IN THE JOB MARKET

Due to fundamental changes in the job market, we are likely to see an increase in workers undertaking short-term, temporary and contract assignments. This will create migratory workforces, which will need to be equipped with basic and key skills for successful participation in a more fluid marketplace. Correspondingly, employers will increasingly expect to use more efficient and effective mechanisms to assess the degree to which potential job candidates possess the required skills. This will increase the pressure on providers of education and training, and other professional development organisations; they will be expected to reshape their vision and activities around these new expectations, which will require new methods of teaching and new methods of assessment. City and Guilds, in their document entitled *Shaping the Workforce of the Future*, make the following statement:

> *The National Skills Task Force has identified that there will be two million additional jobs in the British economy by 2010. Up to 90 per cent of these new jobs will be skilled roles that demand abilities described as at level 2 (equivalent to five GCSEs) or above. Bearing in mind that there will be 700,000 fewer young people in the UK in 2010 than there were in 1999, the jobs will have to be filled from the adult workforce, a third of whom – around nine million – lack level 2 qualifications. Also, given that one in five adults has literacy and numeracy problems, a huge effort is required to turn this situation around.*
>
> *(City and Guilds, 2001)*

EXPECTATIONS OF STUDENTS AND WORKERS

As students and employees are increasingly required to apply their ICT knowledge and skills in centres, colleges and places of work, they will expect educational establishments to provide and deliver training and assessment facilities using modern ICT-based services. Increasing familiarity with, and use of, the internet, communications and personal computing, will make it possible for an individual remotely to select courses that more directly meet their personal learning needs and style. Individuals will increasingly seek opportunities to subscribe to training facilities that offer a more modular, efficient and flexible approach to learning and assessment. As students increasingly learn within, and are surrounded by, a technological world, they will not want to become disadvantaged if forced to undergo more traditional, paper-based assessments. Chapter 2 by Shirley Clarke (page 15), Chapter 3 by Ronald Gallimore and James Stigler (page 25) and Chapter 9 by Stephen Heppell (page 105) make clear that particular forms of technology offer the learner greater freedoms and flexibility than more traditional assessment systems afford.

CHANGES IN POPULATION GROUPS

Increased demand for wider access to personalised learning will not come from workers only. Education is becoming an increasingly popular leisure activity, particularly among older generations, and is the fastest growing sector of consumer spending in the UK. This view is put forward in a Foresight publication (www.foresight.gov.uk) entitled *The Learning Process in 2020: Point and Click – Learners in the Driving Seat*. The article goes on to say that:

> *Given the demographic changes that are expected to take place in the next 30 years, it is reasonable to assume that this market will continue to grow. By 2008, there will be more people of pensionable age than children under 16 in the UK. The number of children is projected to fall by 6.5 per cent to 11.3 million in 2011. In the same period, the population over pensionable age will increase 11 per cent to 11.9 million. Longer term, this figure could reach*

*around 16 million by 2040. [These figures are taken from the government actuary's
department's 1998-based national population projections.]*

(Foresight: Learning in 2020 Task Force, 2001)

EFFECTIVE USE OF TEACHING STAFF

To make more effective use of experienced teachers, trainers and markers in the
future, educational establishments will increasingly look to technology to release skilled
individuals from routine work that could instead be automated.

INCREASING COMPETITION IN THE ASSESSMENT MARKET

Organisations involved in delivering education and assessment services will face
increasing competition from other providers of learning who have already begun to
harness the opportunities presented by ICT. This can be seen by a rise in managed
learning environments (MLEs), such as those provided by Granada, Reed Publishing
(now Harcourt Education), Pearson Education and Research Machines (RM). Others,
such as the British Broadcasting Corporation (BBC) and Channel 4, are seeking to
harness the strengths of digital television with web-based learning materials. These
organisations may traditionally have been based in publications and communications
but now see commercial opportunities to market a whole range of educational
material related to national curriculum tests, public examinations and other
qualifications. MLEs are increasingly likely to add to their provision of 'content'
services by offering ICT-based self-assessment tools that can be used at home. In fact,
high street computer shops already sell a number of software packages that do this (for
example, the Theory Driving Test). Organisations will want to exploit their expertise
to meet the demands of learners and students who themselves seek increasing choice
and convenience in their progression through the learning chain (for example,
choosing the right course, methods of learning, time-frames for learning, locations for
learning, time-frames for assessment, and flexible routes towards certification and
accreditation).

THE 'COPYCAT' EFFECT

A knock-on or 'copycat' effect may occur based on successful ICT-based initiatives
already implemented. For example, the computerisation of the Learner Driver Theory
Test model could be adapted to other test scenarios with the confidence of previous
successful implementations. This creates a positive aura of ICT usage, where success
encourages further success. Already a number of vocational tests, such as the
Construction Industry Training Board (CITB) health and safety tests, are offered
through the Driving Standards Testing centres.

FURTHER TECHNOLOGICAL DEVELOPMENTS

Further developments are likely in the areas of: internet and intranet (for example,
improved security); knowledge management; communications and networks (for
example, increasing bandwidth and connectivity); imaging technology; advanced
man/machine interfaces; more complex control systems; sophisticated modelling and
graphics environments; and rapid software development tools. These technological
developments could all provide opportunities to make the assessment process more
efficient, effective, secure and reliable.

CHANGING THE APPROACH TO TESTING

Traditionally, technology has helped organisations to change *how* they do things but, increasingly, it enables us to question the value of *what* we are doing. For example, in a traditional paper-based assessment, evaluation of a student may be restricted to the limitations of the paper medium because it constrains the scope and nature of the test. Using more sophisticated technology tools, we can create real-world models and 3-D images that allow assessment of a much wider range of skills and abilities. In fact, the way in which a student interacts with these models may yield much more information about the student's capabilities, in contrast to simply achieving a correct answer. The case for this is made by Stephen Heppell in Chapter 9 (page 105); the World Class Arena project has already taken significant steps in the direction of leading us to rethink and redesign tests that are built around the new technologies so that test results become increasingly information-rich. This new paradigm may require a mind-shift away from the more traditional paper-based test approach, but the new technologies could open up exciting opportunities that radically alter our approach to testing and the assessment of its outcomes.

Potential barriers to technological change

Although future technologies may present increasing opportunities to deploy ICT in assessment, there may be a number of potential barriers that could prevent or slow down initiatives in this direction. These potential barriers, none of which are insurmountable, are discussed below.

THE ASSESSMENT PROCESS

The main issues that may prevent faster take-up of ICT facilities to support the processes in the assessment model are:

- The current assessment process is predicated on designing tests and examinations where the reliability, accuracy and consistency of the outcomes rely on the post-examination awarding process.

- The current design of the paper-based test is not always suitable for conversion to on-screen presentation.

- It is difficult to design an equitable ICT-based test that is required to operate in parallel with an existing paper-based test, particularly in cases where multiple-choice or single-answer questions have not been employed in the paper-based test.

- The design and nature of the paper-based test may not easily permit automated marking by a computer.

- It is difficult to set pass/fail mark thresholds in advance, and this would be necessary for automated computer marking and fast turnaround of results to candidates.

- For summative 'high stakes' tests and examinations, there is a lack of IT infrastructure to support reliable and consistent delivery of on-screen tests.

- There is also a lack of IT infrastructure to support on-screen marking at marking centres or by markers at home.

- There is a lack of sufficient skills to change the current modes of assessment, particularly in area of ICT test design.

- The suggestion that 'whole paper' marking might be replaced by a combination of automated marking, clerical marking and expert marking, with the expert marker being unable to take a holistic view of the candidate's performance, is a cause for concern.

- There is a lack of appropriate resources within the regulating bodies to monitor and audit ICT-based assessment.

- The existence of patents for some automated assessment processes may deter others from implementing similar technology-based solutions unless they are prepared to agree to possible licensing demands.

TECHNOLOGY AND INFRASTRUCTURE
Different technological and data infrastructures

Lack of standardised technical infrastructure across the assessment industry will limit opportunities for implementing more strategic initiatives throughout the assessment system. This hits particularly the areas of data collection, data processing, data transmission and receipt. Without a common, efficient and reliable communications infrastructure to route and transmit assessment data, it will be difficult for those involved in the process to operate, manage and share information across the different communication interfaces or environments.

Inadequacy of operational security and reliability

QCA's recent pilot study for ICT assessment in basic and key skills found inconsistency between different organisations in their ability to provide adequate levels of operational security and reliability of assessment services. Concerns about adequate validation of the identity of the candidate and the reliability of computer equipment during an online test, may both work against the development of ICT-based assessments. However, further advances in biometric systems, such as facial recognition, fingerprints, hand-geometry, voice recognition and retinal scans, may offer effective solutions to the candidate validation issues. Equally, failsafe dual-processing systems could be implemented: a 'mirrored' back-up system will automatically take over when the primary system fails or becomes overloaded.

Different pace of technological take-up

Each organisation will embrace technology at a different pace dependent on the internal and external drivers affecting the organisation and the resources and expertise it has at its disposal. This will position organisations differently in their ability to capitalise on and implement new ICT-based opportunities.

Costs associated with full-scale operational implementation

The initial development and implementation costs associated with ICT-based assessments will be high. Outgoings will include fees for the design of new ICT-based tests, administration and delivery software, hardware, communications infrastructure, back-up and recovery facilities, training and ongoing maintenance costs. The paybacks on the larger-scale investments needed to achieve implementation are not likely to be realised in the short to medium term.

MANAGING POLITICAL AND PUBLIC OPINION

A major challenge will be potential cultural resistance to further technological change. Individuals who remain unconvinced about the benefits of ICT will need more immediate proof of ICT's ability to deliver benefits, and may not be prepared to wait for them to accrue over the medium to long term. By its very nature, the assessment community is risk averse, and will therefore want to proceed with any change to the current assessment mechanisms with a high degree of caution. The political and public reaction to failures in the assessment process, particularly with regard to the high stakes examinations (for example, GCSEs and A/AS levels) is of great concern. Consequently, whilst ICT-based assessment pilots may be relatively low risk, the commitment and confidence needed to scale up the pilot studies for full-scale implementations may be considerable.

Analysing the benefits of ICT

A number of perceived benefits are often quoted relating to the deployment of ICT in assessment. In reality, the extent to which some or all of these benefits might be realised will depend very much on the particular assessment process to which ICT is applied. Clearly, any benefits that may improve the assessment process will have to be offset by the associated ICT development and other resource costs that would be incurred.

In Tables 5.1 and 5.2 on pages 63 and 64, each perceived benefit has been categorised as being either a benefit of 'efficiency' (Table 5.1) or a benefit of 'effectiveness' (Table 5.2). Efficiency is related to the timeliness of the assessment service, speed of processing and operation, whereas effectiveness relates to the quality and reliability of the assessment itself, its service delivery and operation. A commentary is provided to give additional insight regarding the context in which the benefit might be realised, and who would be its primary recipient.

Table 5.1: *Perceived efficiency (time) benefits*

PERCEIVED BENEFIT	PRIMARY BENEFICIARY
Rapid testing of a wide range of knowledge This will depend on the scope of the assessment, the way it is delivered and the time allocated for the test. If the on-screen test is adaptive it can take account of the ability and performance of the candidate and eliminate the presentation of unnecessary questions. The test time allocated can then be used to deliver questions tailored to the candidate's ability or to test additional topics and subject areas. Health and safety standards recommend limits to the time spent in front of a computer monitor, and also advocate intervening rest periods, so length of test is an important issue.	Candidate
Efficiency through reduction in marker time, leading to a reduction in teacher workload Reduction in teacher workload will only occur if the teacher is also a marker. Marker workload will only reduce where ICT is used to automatically mark some or all test questions, or where it is used to electronically distribute less difficult test questions for on-screen marking by less experienced or 'clerical' markers.	Test provider
Availability 'on demand' for cohorts and for individual learners On-demand tests will be available where there are sufficient test questions in an online item bank to allow continuous delivery of tests without the possibility of the same questions reappearing too frequently.	Test provider
An item bank can be updated continuously, without the need to send new test versions to users A central computer data bank of test items can be used to electronically download subsets of questions to a centre for a specific test on a specific day. Centralisation will improve the overall control of test items and improve the efficiency of test distribution to centres.	Test provider
Flexible access by learners, including small groups being tested in minority subjects or students who are geographically dispersed (leading to improved test availability in remote locations) With regard to summative assessment, undertaking a test using ICT from a remote location still raises the issue of adequate invigilation and quality of the test delivery when compared to the more controlled environment of a test centre.	Candidate
Using ICT brings cost benefits to awarding bodies and others in the assessment system Whilst there are potential cost savings to be derived from print and distribution, markers and administration, these are offset in the early years by IT infrastructure investment, software development and investment in training.	Test provider

From Tables 5.1 and 5.2 (see above and overleaf), it appears that most of the ICT related benefits of efficiency accrue to the test providers, whereas ICT benefits relating to quality are largely enjoyed by candidates. This is perhaps not surprising given that the providers of assessment services will be keen to maximise efficiency and minimise their costs. Candidates will want quality and reliability in the assessment instrument itself (as will assessment providers), as well as quality in relation to test delivery, although speed will be important in the feedback of results.

Table 5.2: *Perceived effectiveness (quality) benefits*

PERCEIVED BENEFIT	PRIMARY BENEFICIARY
Rapid testing of a wide range of knowledge This will depend on the scope of the assessment, the way it is delivered and the time allocated for the test. If the on-screen test is adaptive it can take account of the ability and performance of the candidate and eliminate the presentation of unnecessary questions. The test time allocated can then be used to deliver questions tailored to the candidate's ability or to test additional topics and subject areas. Health and safety standards recommend limits to the time spent in front of a computer monitor, and also advocate intervening rest periods, so length of test is an important issue.	Candidate
Immediate feedback for pupils on learning styles from formative assessment This may be realised where ICT is used not only to mark an assessment but where it also monitors and then analyses the student's interaction with the assessment or learning situation.	Candidate
Reliability of assessment On-screen assessment can offer certain types of questions and enable test developers to make use of multimedia. Multimedia technology may allow test designers to assess capabilities that they cannot assess using paper-based tests. In some subjects this may make the assessment instrument increasingly fit for purpose and therefore more reliable. In addition, reliability will be highest where more objective marking can be applied to a question, particularly where there is a clear-cut 'right' answer. Automatic computer marking for these objective question types leads to consistency of marking and fairness for the candidate.	Candidate
Greater capacity for self-assessment and for students to monitor their own learning This will be the case where there are sufficient test questions in the item bank to permit the candidate to undertake practice attempts prior to the real test (e.g. the Driving Theory Test offers this facility). Practice sessions will increase the opportunity for the student to quickly identify areas of weakness, correct them and be assessed as soon as they feel ready.	Candidate
ICT used in assessment might also motivate candidates Motivation will be increased where the quality of the assessment design, the test delivery and the test environment is high.	Candidate
Sophisticated feedback for pupils on learning styles from formative assessment Improved feedback may be provided where ICT is used to mark an assessment and provide feedback of results at a detailed level, and also where it monitors and then analyses the student's interaction with the assessment or learning situation.	Candidate
Privacy and non-judgemental feedback for less confident learners This may be realised where ICT is used not only to mark an assessment but also to monitor and then analyse the student's interaction with the assessment or learning situation, and to provide feedback direct to the learner.	Candidate
Candidate answers can be sent automatically to a central server, enabling continuous monitoring of the performance of questions as well as of the individuals Continuous monitoring could be beneficial to a student where ICT is designed to deliver more difficult or easier questions dependent on the performance of the candidate in the test so far (i.e. the test is adaptive). Continuous monitoring of questions in real-time by a centre or awarding body would only be beneficial if there was a potential need for removing the question while a test was in progress. However, if an item bank was being used, it would enable the awarding body to manage the bank more effectively and remove poorly performing questions quickly.	Candidate Test provider
Assessment using ICT reflects candidate learning styles and experience Learners are increasingly using technology as an integral part of the way they learn: pencil-and-paper tests will become increasingly alien to them.	Candidate
Accuracy and consistency of assessment The use of computer-marked assessment and the introduction of ICT into more areas of the assessment process could lead to outcomes that are more accurate and consistent through the elimination of human error and subjectivity.	Test provider

Conclusion

This chapter describes the main stages in the assessment process and identifies where ICT can be applied still further to achieve improvements in both efficiency and effectiveness. Although ICT already supports a number of assessment stages, it is not particularly widespread in the areas of electronic test distribution to centres, on-screen delivery to the candidate or automated marking by computer. The extent to which ICT can pervade these assessment processes may depend less on what technology has to offer in the future, and more on our ability and willingness to move away from the more traditional paper-based approaches that have served us for so long.

6

Making technology count in formative and summative assessment

Alastair Walker

Northern Ireland Council for the Curriculum, Examinations and Assessment (CCEA), Belfast, UK

Introduction

A GROUP OF PROFESSIONALS involved in the promotion of educational technology were asked to consider the changes of the last 10 years in relation to their expectations of change. They all agreed that the advances in technology had exceeded their expectations by far, but the *rate* at which the use of technology in schools had increased had fallen well *below* them. The long-predicted technological revolution in education has not yet materialised. Our grandparents would not feel entirely out of place in many modern classrooms, although there are clear signs that this will not remain the case for much longer.

In the 1990s, information technology (IT) became information and communications technology (ICT) and it is the *communication* rather than the *computing* potential of recent developments that is beginning to create real change in teaching and learning. The combination of broadband connection, digital imaging and mobile telephony will undoubtedly transform every student's life over the forthcoming decade. The challenge will be to ensure that there is real educational gain from the changes that take place.

Multimedia resources to assist learning are becoming ever more commonplace and valued in many areas of the curriculum. Little attention, however, has been paid to the application of technology in assessment or in formal examinations. Perhaps the most acute example of the disparity can be seen in recently introduced tests to assess competence in the use of computers as part of the key skills qualification. These are pencil-and-paper tests. It seems bizarre to attempt to measure computer skills through a written test, but at present the capability of providing such tests online is still in development.

The Northern Ireland Council for the Curriculum, Examinations and Assessment (CCEA) has been working on two projects that are designed to make progress in

67

applying new technology to assessment and examinations. In one case the focus is the 'high stakes' public examination: the Paperless Examinations Project. In the other it is formative assessment in the classroom: the Assessment for Learning Project. Although there are elements of the two projects that overlap, particularly in the presentation of computer-based tasks to students, there are also substantial differences – because of the different contexts within which the technology will be used. The security considerations surrounding high stakes public examinations, for instance, create a particular set of constraints that are absent from day-to-day assessment in the classroom.

The Paperless Examination Project

The Paperless Examination Project (PEP) began in 2000 with an agreement between Edexcel and CCEA to collaborate on a development project. A scoping study was carried out early that year in order to establish the nature of the project and the extent to which relevant work was being done elsewhere. In fact there was little evidence at that time of similar work being undertaken in Europe, although computer-based testing was becoming quite common in the USA. The main difference between the tests being delivered on screen in America and in UK public examinations was the use of automated marking. The nature of subject-based public examinations is such that many of the students' answers require marking by professional markers; the marking cannot be entirely automated.

PHASE 1

A Project Officer took up post in October 2000 and the partners engaged the services of NCS Pearson as software developer for Phase 1 of the project. In Phase 1 it was decided to conduct a small-scale trial, in schools in Northern Ireland, of a test similar in nature to those used in science examinations of the General Certificate of Secondary Education (GCSE). In fact, the decision was taken to use only question types *already in use* in written examinations. This meant that a control group of students was able to take the same test on paper as was being trialled on computer. It also meant that, in the first phase, the issues being addressed were essentially technological rather than educational and two different sets of issues were not then confounded in the trial.

Full details of the Phase 1 trial and its outcomes are contained in the published report (CCEA, 2001) and so only a brief outline will be given here, followed by a discussion of the principal issues to emerge and how these are being taken forward in the second phase of the project. The schools chosen for the trial all had a relatively well-developed infrastructure, including a local area intranet. External connection was via ISDN lines. There were difficulties within the trial as a result of technological limitations in some of the schools. There were also problems in matching the software being used in the project (mostly adapted from applications in USA) to the systems being used in schools and in CCEA. Nonetheless, in the spring of 2001 five science tests were run in six schools; the student responses were marked using a combination of automated and professional marking.

These first trials demonstrated the feasibility of conducting a formal examination on computer on a very limited scale. Most of the students involved reacted positively, although some would have preferred to take the test on paper. When the results from the computer- and paper-based tests were compared it was found that those taking the tests on paper had performed better in each case than those taking them on computer. The differences, however, were not marked and were not statistically significant.

PHASE 2

Phase 2 of the project is now taking place, with further trials planned for early 2003 in a selection of schools in Northern Ireland and in England. The software supplier in Phase 2 is Bradford Technology Ltd. and the tests to be trialled will be in science and in geography. In this phase, the potential of the computer will be explored to enhance the examinations by presenting tasks in a way that would not be possible on paper. The choice of subjects is quite important in this respect.

Science

Science was chosen for the first trial because tests in science for 16 year olds typically contain some questions where the marking can be automated, along with others that require professional marking. A paper-based test of this nature must be entirely professionally marked. When carried out on computer, it is easily possible to arrange for some responses to be computer-marked and some to be given to professional markers. This has advantages for the examination system, which at present is experiencing difficulty in recruiting sufficient numbers of markers. Science also had the advantage in the first trial of not being demanding of students in terms of the amount of keying: normally, science tests at this level only require short-sentence responses at the most. It is not yet possible to expect all students to have sufficiently well-developed keyboard skills to tackle an English or history examination on-screen.

Science is also included in the second trial for much the same reasons, but also because of the opportunity it provides to make use of the potential of the computer in presenting material. Animated graphics or video clips can create a virtual laboratory that allows a much more process-based approach to assessment. Environmental and industrial aspects of science can be explored more realistically.

Geography

The same is also true of geography. Candidates can go on virtual field trips while taking their examination. Geographical phenomena can be presented in action rather than just diagrammatically. High quality graphic images can be used to expand the range of geographical understanding that the examination addresses.

In Phase 2 we will only begin to explore this potential in these two subjects. The possibilities in other subjects are, perhaps, even more far-reaching.

ISSUES ARISING FROM THE PROJECT

The issues that emerged from PEP in the first trials illustrated many of the problems that will have to be overcome before a fully computer-based system of public examinations can be introduced. Only when the National Grid for Learning, which is intended to be the UK's major step-up in interconnectivity, is fully in place will it be possible to consider a major system-change of this nature. Even then, it will not be possible simply to transfer the current paper-based system onto computer. Logistics alone would prevent that.

Test delivery and administration

On the days when large examinations for the General Certificate of Secondary Education (GCSE) are taking place each June, up to 625,000 candidates are sitting examinations at the same time. That will not be possible if those examinations are being taken on computer. A different system will be required to allow much smaller numbers of students to be taking examinations at any given time. This has large-scale implications for school organisation and for the examination system itself. There are also smaller-scale issues that need to be addressed. Examinations are conducted in silence and in a way that ensures that one candidate cannot see the responses of any other candidates. Maintaining the same level of security and of silence in a computer suite may be challenging. There are ways in which the security question can be dealt with, but keyboards are not silent. However, there is potential to use sound in the computer-presentation of examination questions. That would require the use of headphones, thus solving the keyboard problem in the process.

Special arrangements

Other issues that emerged in the trial included the question of special arrangements for students with disabilities. Some candidates, because of the nature of their disabilities, find it easier to work on computer than on paper. For others it might make little difference, but for some the computer-based examination may be much more difficult to cope with. Currently, examination papers are prepared in Braille for blind candidates. It is not at all clear how the type of computer-based examination described above, incorporating animated graphics or video clips, could be made accessible to blind or even partially-sighted candidates. If sound is also used, those with hearing impairments would be excluded. These are matters that need to be addressed early in the development process and not left to be considered as an afterthought.

Use of time

The question of the use of time in the examination is one that the trial candidates raised in the evaluation. Although indicators were provided on screen of the elapsed time, and of the number of questions remaining, candidates found that they were unable to gain the sense of the wholeness of the test, and their position in it, as they did with a paper-based test. The facility to scroll back and forward through questions does not generate the same sense of wholeness as flicking through a question booklet. Perhaps this is an issue simply of unfamiliarity with the medium and it will be resolved as students gain greater experience of working through computer-based tests.

Postscript

It is important to note by way of a postscript that the PEP has not, so far, been experimenting with online examinations. In the Phase 1 trial, the examination software was downloaded to servers within the schools. The individual computers used by the candidates were networked only to these servers. Once the examination was completed the software, now including candidate responses, was uploaded from the schools to the central examination server. It is felt that where candidates take examinations online through the internet, there is a risk of systems failure; this method reduces that risk.

IMPLICATIONS OF CHANGE

In looking forward to the possibility of the public examination system in the UK becoming computer-based, it is necessary to recognise that the change would have substantial educational implications. As explained earlier, we must ensure that any change of this nature will bring *educational gain* as well as *improved efficiency*. The educational gain will include the changed nature of examinations; more importantly, changing examinations will also have a 'backwash' effect on the curriculum. Teachers do 'teach to the test'. One of the factors currently limiting the benefits that teachers can get from the use of technology is the fact that the benefits do not translate to the examination room. Once that is no longer the case, teachers will be encouraged to ensure that the learning experience of students reflects the way that technology is used in the examinations.

Michael Kingdon (see Chapter 8), when Head of Research for the University of London Schools Examination Board, discovered in the archives a record of the first matriculation examination in chemistry – conducted by the Board in the mid-nineteenth century (Kingdon, 1990). The examination was completed in a single day, beginning with the writing of the questions by the examiners early in the morning and finishing with the posting of the results on the noticeboard that afternoon. Nowadays the process is much longer, stretching out over two years, but otherwise has changed remarkably little. Moving to a computer-based system will be the greatest upheaval in public examinations since they began. It will take some time and will require simultaneous changes by examination boards, schools, colleges and others over a considerable period of time. The regulatory authorities will have to alter the regulatory framework governing the conduct of examinations in order to allow the change to take place. Such a programme will only be successfully managed if it is based upon a coherent long-term strategy.

The CCEA Assessment for Learning Project

AIMS

In their review of literature relating to the impact of formative assessment, Black and Wiliam (1998b) refer to research that demonstrates just how much good-quality feedback to students improves their learning. They present evidence that the award of grades or marks does not have the impact of clear descriptive responses by the teacher that inform the student of strengths and weaknesses and point to the next steps to be taken. In this sense, assessment should be seen as an activity *contributing* to learning, rather than simply *describing* what has been achieved. The first aim of the CCEA Assessment for Learning Project is to provide *computer-based methods of classroom assessment* that facilitate good quality feedback and, at the same time, contribute to the second aim of the project, which is to facilitate the keeping of *records of students' work*, which will later form the basis of summative reports.

The project began in April 2001 as part of a programme of projects funded through HM Treasury's Invest to Save Budget via a consortium of the regulatory authorities led by QCA. The software for the project is provided by ALTA Systems of Belfast. Initially the project is focusing on mathematics and English but an increase in the scope of the project is planned so that it will eventually cover all areas of the curriculum.

The statutory curriculum and assessment arrangements in Northern Ireland are currently under review. Changes are due to be phased in from September 2004 onwards. In the revised curriculum it is intended that there will be greater emphasis than at present on transferable skills and competences. A central spine of transferable skills has been devised, around which the programmes for the different curriculum areas have been built. The place of personal development, including personal, social and health education (PSHE), citizenship and work-related education, has been strengthened. It is intended that the development work in assessment will reflect these changes.

COMPUTER-BASED METHODS OF CLASSROOM ASSESSMENT

The software being developed includes a wide variety of question authoring and question answering devices, thus allowing a substantial diversity of tasks to be included. Where it is feasible to do so, automated marking is used. Scope for professional assessment by the teacher is provided where required. Two further features are in development. These are the use of adaptive assessment and the creation of exemplar libraries.

Adaptive or 'formative' assessment takes place when the computer is programmed to select questions from a question bank at a level of difficulty determined by the student's responses. This in itself can be employed as helpful feedback as the student works, but only in contexts where automated marking is feasible. Exemplar libraries, on the other hand, are of benefit in contexts requiring professional assessment by the teacher. The libraries contain work that has previously been assessed, with all of the assessor's comments included. Students can use the libraries to help them to see exactly what the teacher will be looking for in assessing the work that is to be done. Teachers can use the libraries in making sure that the assessment is fair and focuses on the important features of the students' work.

Curriculum links

In order for a computer-based classroom assessment system to be of use, it must be systematically linked to the statutory curriculum that the teacher is following. Teachers should also find it easy to match the material on the system to their schemes of work. In the initial development work done on the project, based on the current statutory curriculum, all the assessment material has been mapped onto that curriculum. A curriculum browser enables teachers to locate in the system material relating to the area of the curriculum on which they are currently working. The assessment tasks can therefore easily be matched to the learning that is taking place in the classroom. When the revised curriculum is introduced, it is intended that it will be accompanied by sample schemes of works that teachers can choose to use if they wish, or to adapt as necessary. The assessment material in the system will then be re-mapped to align with the revised curriculum and the browser adapted to match the sample schemes of work.

Online delivery

As this assessment system (unlike the PEP) is not being designed to operate in the high stakes public examination context, there is not the same need to build in security requirements, or to be concerned to the same degree with system failure. Initial trials of the system are therefore being conducted using a central server accessed by students working online. At present, technological limitations mean that loading times are long, leading to some frustration among students and teachers. Broadband connections will resolve that issue.

Formative and summative feedback

As has already been noted, high quality feedback is most important if the system is to meet its aim. This can be achieved through automated marking (for example in mathematics) if the system is capable of reporting in qualitative terms the strengths and weaknesses that have characterised the work done by the student. One way in which reporting will be assisted is through the facility to replay to the students each step of their work, in order to identify the mistakes that may have led to wrong answers. Such a process would have a particular value in student self-assessment. Where teacher assessment is used, comments will be provided directly on the quality of the work.

RECORDS OF STUDENTS' WORK

As well as providing formative feedback at the time the work is done, it is also intended that the system will incorporate means of recording assessment outcomes in a readily accessible 'summative' form for future reference. The recording system will reflect the curriculum mapping already described and will be capable of holding information about work done by students other than that which has been completed on the computer. Indeed, it will be possible for teachers to note important aspects of the work of students that they have observed in the classroom, or that have become evident in classroom discussions. At present, early developmental work on the recording system is also being carried out – on the basis of records being held on the central server and accessed online. A registration system limits access by students to their own records only and by teachers to the records of their own students only.

Replacing the markbook

In effect, the recording system will replace the traditional teacher's markbook. The potential of the computer to sort and hold information will be exploited to create a resource that is richer and more systematically linked to the curriculum than most traditional markbooks. Several teachers will be contributing simultaneously to the record of an individual student. In some cases, these contributions will be independent, in that they will relate to different curriculum areas: in other situations (in the case of transferable skills, for example), different teachers will be contributing to a common record. At present the contribution of a number of teachers to a common record is difficult to achieve and very time consuming. In designing an electronic markbook, the challenge is to achieve an educational gain in the richness of the record, while permitting no increase in the workload of teachers. In fact, there ought to be considerable potential to use computers to achieve reduction in teacher workload in the whole area of recording and reporting.

School reports

In most schools at the beginning of the twenty-first century, the school report is produced in exactly the same manner as was used at the end of the nineteenth century. A *pro forma* for each student in a class is passed between all the teachers who teach the class. Should the last contributor to a report make a serious error, all the other teachers have to fill out the *pro forma* a second time. Such an antiquated process is crying out for computer assistance. Provided all teachers are content to key in comments (and at present that is probably not the case), it would be possible with current technology to set up a template on computer and produce all reports through a computerised system. Indeed some schools are doing so already. Bringing together a computerised system of student records, carefully mapped to the curriculum, with a system of computer-based report generation, has enormous potential to improve the quality of reports as well as reduce the amount of work involved in producing them.

Creating a system of student records matched to one for the generation of reports to parents – and all linked to the revised statutory curriculum now being devised in Northern Ireland and the accompanying sample schemes of work – will contribute to the second aim of the Assessment for Learning Project. One byproduct of such a system would be the facility to collect data at class, year group, school or whole cohort level for evaluation or benchmarking purposes. Northern Ireland no longer publishes school performance tables, but it is still considered important that performance data are available to measure the level of progress in the education service as a whole and to provide schools with the opportunity for self-evaluation through benchmarking.

PRIORITIES

In the first instance, however, the primary aim of the project takes precedence: to produce a computer-based assessment system that has real formative power. Initial trials have been undertaken in some schools in Northern Ireland. The results indicate a very positive reaction by both teachers and students to the assessment process in mathematics. Initial indications are that the system devised for assessment of writing in English may be over-complex and will require significant simplification. This work is at too early a stage for there to be any published reports, but evaluation is being conducted by the Graduate School of Education in Queen's University, Belfast.

Conclusion

The two projects described above represent, to some extent, alternative solutions to the same problem – the introduction of computer power into educational assessment. They remain distinct and each is viable in its own right because there is likely to be a continuing need for externally marked tests carried out under secure conditions in the context of the award of qualifications. On the other hand, the assessment of younger students in particular is likely to be largely based on day-to-day classroom work and the Assessment for Learning Project is focused mainly on the primary context and lower secondary.

Each of the two solutions has the potential to have a dramatic effect on the teaching and learning process in classrooms. If so, there are issues of great importance regarding the preparation of teachers in terms of initial teacher training and also their continuing professional development. There have been significant developments in recent years, including the training of teachers, through the New Opportunities Fund, in the use of ICT. The focus of that training was increasing the use of computers as a curriculum resource.

The pace at which change takes place will depend on the pace at which teachers can themselves make the transition to a working life that is largely computer based. At present teachers are unusual as professionals in that computers tend to be marginal to their working life rather than central. The great majority of teachers do not log on daily to a computer that is set aside for their personal use, even if the machines are employed to some degree in the classroom context. Schools are among the last institutions for whom most internal communication is on paper.

The long-predicted revolution in education caused by the introduction of new technology has failed to materialise. So long as examinations require use of pen and paper, and so long as formative assessment in the classroom is likewise fixed in its traditional methods, the revolution can only be a limited one. Educational gain must be demonstrable for change to be justified. That gain is most likely to emerge if curriculum and assessment are transformed as one.

7 The Qualified Teacher Status Skills Tests: lessons learned and plans for the future

Angela Walsh
Teacher Training Agency, London, UK

Introduction

IN DECEMBER 1998, AS PART OF A PROGRAMME TO MODERNISE TEACHING and improve the status of the profession, the Secretary of State for Education in England published a Green Paper entitled *Teachers: Meeting the Challenge of Change* (GB.DfEE, 1998b). This contained a number of proposed developments for the education system in England, generally in relation to schools, but also focusing on initial teacher training (ITT). One of these proposals was for the introduction of tests for trainee teachers. Passing the tests would form part of the requirements for gaining Qualified Teacher Status (QTS), a necessary qualification for those wishing to take up teaching posts in maintained schools and non-maintained special schools. Earlier in 1998, the Government had set out requirements for a core curriculum for ITT in English, mathematics, science and information and communications technology (ICT) (GB.DfEE, 1998a). The intended purpose of both of these reforms was to further improve the quality of new teachers entering the profession.

In July 1999 the Teacher Training Agency (TTA), a non-departmental government body responsible for improving teacher recruitment and training quality, was asked to take forward this work on behalf of the Department for Education and Skills (DfES) by developing Skills Tests. These were to cover three specific areas of competence – literacy, numeracy and ICT – and were to be introduced from summer 2000 onwards.

Setting up the project

Work on the Qualified Teacher Status Skills Tests began in July 1999 when the TTA set about the task of scoping the project requirements and taking advice from many groups representing the teaching profession – especially those involved in teacher training. The tests were to be a requirement, but their operation should not impose an added burden on any group involved in working with trainee teachers – whether in schools, universities or colleges.

AIMS OF THE TESTS

The national curricula for ITT (GB.DfEE, 1998a), included a set of standards to be met by trainee teachers which incorporated the professional use of the three skill areas. However, the Office for Standards in Education (OfSTED) for England provided evidence indicating that the capability of newly qualified teachers for making use of their skills in literacy, numeracy and ICT was not as high as expected. Teachers, perhaps more than other professionals, are by the nature of their work under continual public scrutiny: the Skills Tests offered the opportunity to provide extra reassurance of new teachers' capabilities. In support of this intention, it was decided that the test material should reflect, as far as possible, the range of real contexts that newly qualified teachers (NQTs) would meet at the start of their careers: success on the tests would demonstrate their competence.

FLEXIBLE AND ACCESSIBLE

The routes into teaching in England involve the standard university or college courses of between one and four years' duration, school-based training programmes and flexible, shortened programmes. There was a need to ensure that the testing requirements could be easily met, regardless of which training route had been followed. To meet this need, to minimise the burden on all involved and to provide maximum choice for all trainee teachers, it was decided that the tests must not only be accessible in terms of where they could be taken, but also readily available throughout the year. Computerised test delivery was the chosen way forward, as it could provide immediate results and feedback as well as meeting the access and flexibility requirement. Furthermore, the ITT requirements specified that the national curriculum for the use of ICT in subject teaching must be taught to *all* trainees on *all* courses. It was widely agreed that a computerised test was the only way forward for the valid testing of these skills.

The number of test attempts that trainee teachers should be allowed was decided following consultation with a range of educationalists. Four attempts would be allowed to pass each of the Skills Tests. This was seen as fair and reasonable, given both the 'high stakes' nature of the tests and the innovative approach to testing adopted.

VALUE FOR MONEY

Ensuring value for money was a key priority for TTA. It was recognised that the development and introduction of computerised tests was likely to be expensive in the first instance, in comparison with the traditional paper-based model; however, it was agreed that the financial benefits of computerised delivery would accrue in the longer term. For example, the computer model provided for security of the test material, and therefore enabled it to be used for longer periods; it also lessened the administration required of the providers.

CONTRACTORS FOR DEVELOPMENT AND DELIVERY

Contractors were appointed for both the test development aspect of the project and the test delivery system, following a tendering process. NCS Pearson was the preferred bidder for the test delivery system. The Oxford, Cambridge and Royal Society of Arts (OCR) awarding body, in partnership with NCS Pearson, was contracted to develop the numeracy test materials; both contracts ran from October 1999. The East London Assessment Group (ELAG) was appointed in January 2000 to develop the literacy test materials and in February 2000 the ICT test development work was contracted to 3T Productions Ltd.

SCHEDULE

Around 100,000 Skills Tests are required for downloading each year to provide for the cohort of trainee teachers who are in their final year; supplying material for this volume of tests presented TTA with a considerable challenge. Although the original plan had been for the tests to be introduced during the summer of 2000, the revised schedule was as follows:

- A national numeracy test in a paper-based format was administered in June 2000 and a second test was held in July 2000, for those who had been unsuccessful in June. The computerised numeracy tests went live in February 2001.

- The computerised literacy tests also went live in February 2001.

- The ICT test was programmed from scratch, and was originally scheduled to go live in February 2001. However, TTA took the decision to postpone the launch for several months in order to test further its technical stability. Since the test bedded down well following its introduction in September 2001, it appears that this was indeed the correct decision, if a difficult one to take at the time.

THE DEVELOPMENT PROCESS

The nature of the Skills Tests necessitated new and creative approaches to development. The test materials were developed using a rigorous test development model that incorporated the use of peer review groups and substantial trialling of questions or units. Pre-tests were carried out with large representative samples to provide the necessary data sets to enable full statistical analyses of test reliability, content validity and bias. The analyses provided for the equating of sets of questions to ensure comparable levels of difficulty. They also provided the basis for the production of benchmark tests used for calibration and equating purposes. These tests were indicative of the standard required and were published on the TTA website.

Numeracy test

The development process for the paper-based numeracy test had to ensure that the model used would integrate effectively into a computerised version to be used from 2001 onwards. This test was, perhaps, the simplest to develop, as it was designed to fit into an established testing package. However, the requirement for a movable calculator, some more complex graphical representations and an audio-delivered mental arithmetic section (see description of test contents on pages 80 to 82) proved to be more of a challenge, since it required the building of new customised software to integrate with the established software.

Literacy test

The literacy test material proved reasonably easy to develop, but the computerisation was less straightforward. The writing team worked closely with specialist software developers to ensure successful interfacing with the test delivery system.

ICT test

The ICT test was by far the most challenging technically to develop. The developers could not use generic software, and therefore had to build totally new software, including applications that would allow the execution of a fixed number of specific functions.

TEST DELIVERY

Following decisions about the test development process, attention was turned to the test delivery model and the provision of the necessary infrastructure to host the test delivery system. At this stage the tests were seen as highly controversial by a good number of ITT providers. Other ITT providers did not have the necessary resources to enable them to host a test centre. The system adopted involved establishing a network of 50 TTA test centres spread throughout England. These were based in a variety of educational settings, with a fair number at ITT provider sites. The 50 centres had to be funded and equipped with all that was required, including the provision of trained administrators for each test centre. Following this initial stage a managing agent was contracted to cover all of the centres.

The delivery system works as follows: candidates register for the tests using a secure website, gain a password, and then book tests at a convenient time at a test centre of their choice, using the web. The tests are downloaded to each site daily, using a secure system, and the test centre administrator uploads the completed tests at the end of each day.

TEST SPECIFICATIONS

The tests were designed to provide a 'pass' or 'fail' result immediately on completion. The candidates would receive their results, addressed to them personally and displayed on-screen. Additional feedback was provided if a candidate had been unsuccessful. Before leaving the test centre, the candidate would receive a computer printout of the information provided on-screen.

Content of the tests

NUMERACY TEST

The numeracy test covers:
• mental arithmetic;
• interpreting and using statistical information;
• using and applying general arithmetic.

The test lasts for around 45 minutes and consists of two parts. It begins with a mental arithmetic section, where candidates hear spoken questions over headphones and have 18 seconds in which to answer each question. The second part of the test comprises

16 on-screen questions covering aspects of interpreting and using statistical information based on real data and on using and applying general arithmetic.

The question items cover multiple-response, multiple-choice and single-answer types and incorporate point-and-click and drag-and-drop facilities. An on-screen calculator is available for use only for the second part of the test. This can be moved around the screen as required.

The question is heard via headphones and repeated and then 18 seconds are available before the question answer box, as shown in Figure 7.1 (below), leaves the screen and the next question begins. Candidates have pencil and paper and may jot down essential information. A practice question precedes the start of this part of the test.

Figure 7.1: *Numeracy Skills Test: mental arithmetic*

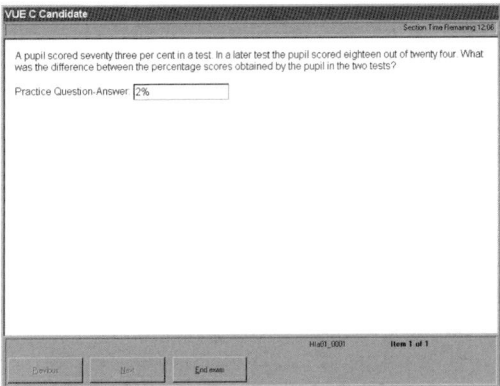

The item shown in Figure 7.2 (below) uses real data about examination results for schools. The question is presented on screen, firstly with a request to click on the question button, which causes the screen shown in Figure 7.2 to be displayed. The calculator key can be seen in the top right-hand position and once on screen can be moved around and used as required. The question is answered by dragging the selected responses to the highlighted positions.

Figure 7.2: *Numeracy Skills Test: school test results, data analysis*

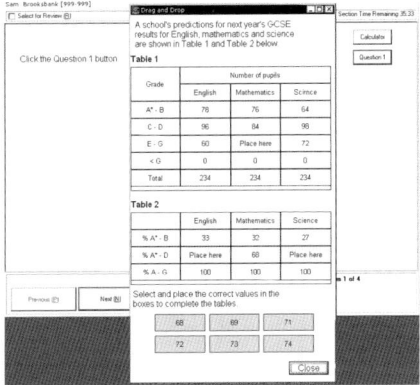

The item shown in Figure 7.3 (below) also uses real data from a number of schools and involves analysis of the spreadsheet data and the identification of the school whose results had not improved over the two-year cycle.

Figure 7.3: *Numeracy Skills Test: examination results data*

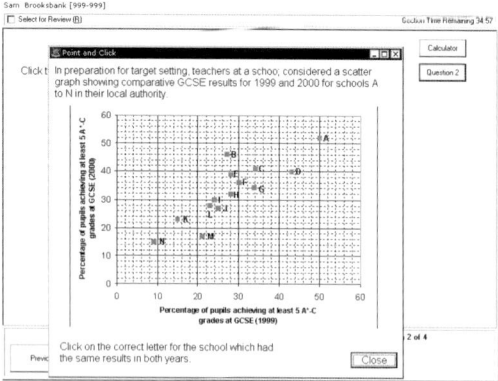

The final numeracy item, shown in Figure 7.4 (below), requires the interpretation of a 'box and whisker' graph showing data about the national results from key stage 2 tests for 11 year olds.

Figure 7.4: *Numeracy Skills Test: interpretation of key stage 2 test data*

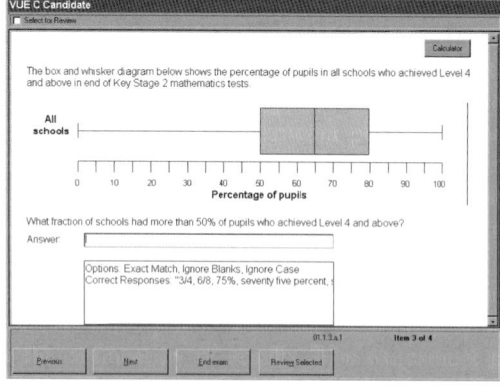

LITERACY TEST

The literacy test covers:
• spelling;
• punctuation;
• comprehension;
• grammar.

Spelling

The spelling element of the test (see Figure 7.5, page 83) is in audio format. A silent multiple-choice version is available for candidates with hearing impairment. Candidates use the headphones provided and can repeat this section, or elements of it, as many times as they wish. However, they must weigh up the time taken for this part against the whole-test maximum time of 45 minutes. The words chosen are ones that all newly-qualified teachers would be expected to know how to spell correctly.

Figure 7.5: *Literacy Skills Test: spelling section*

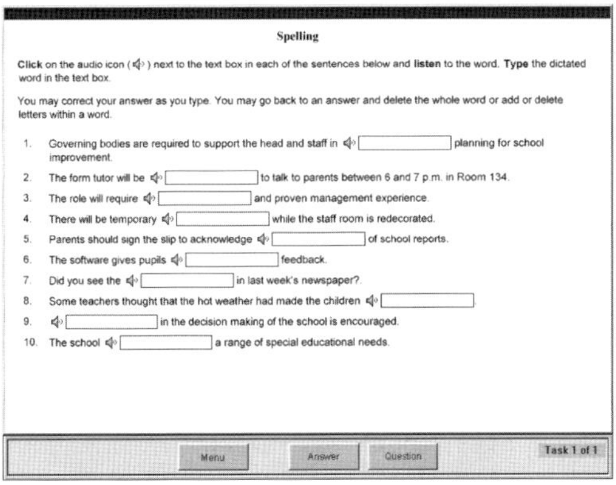

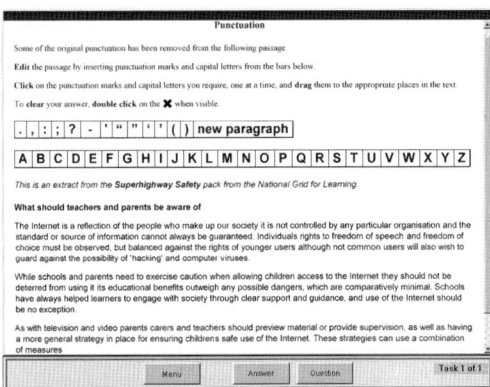

Punctuation test

The punctuation passages provided (see Figure 7.6, below) are drawn from teaching-related educational material, which has been punctuated only partly. Candidates are required to supply the missing punctuation so that it is consistent with that which is already shown. Candidates are made aware in the support materials that the test passages contain a number of points at which punctuation can be inserted, even though it may not be needed. To respond to this section, candidates need to drag punctuation marks and capital letters into each paragraph.

Figure 7.6: *Literacy Skills Test: punctuation section*

Comprehension and grammar tests

The comprehension and grammar sections use test material from a range of educational websites that NQTs are likely to encounter in their work. Candidates are asked to respond to a number of different types of questions related to the given text/s. Answering the questions usually involves using a point-and-click or drag-and-drop facility, or the insertion of single numbers.

For *comprehension* the different types of questions that are used include, amongst others:
• attributing statements to categories;
• completing a bulleted list;
• sequencing information;
• presenting main points;
• identifying the meaning of words;
• evaluating statements about the text.

The material used in the example (see Figure 7.7, below) relates to a research project on improving primary schools; this can be found on the local education authority section of the DfES website.

Figure 7.7: *Literacy Skills Test: comprehension section*

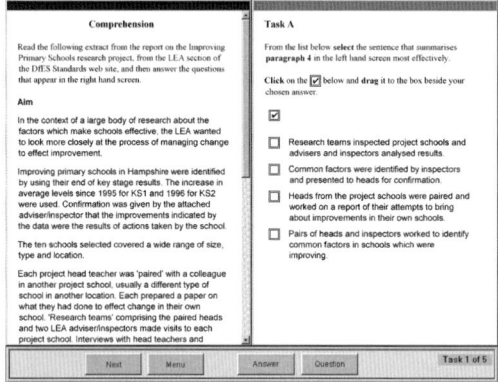

Figure 7.8: *Literacy Skills Test: grammar section*

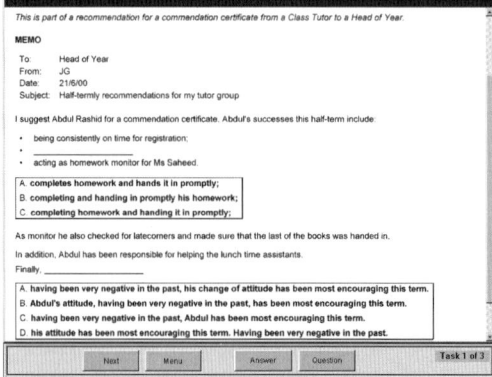

The *grammar* section (see Figure 7.8, above) assesses the candidates' knowledge of standard written English and their ability to use it unambiguously. It also assesses their ability to select a written style consistent with a given text. The text material used in this example relates to the pastoral aspect of the teacher's role.

ICT TEST

The coverage of the ICT test is as shown in Table 7.1.

Table 7.1: *ICT Skills Test, applications and skill areas*

APPLICATIONS	SKILL AREAS
Word processor	Researching and categorising information
Web browser	
Database	Presenting and communicating information
Spreadsheet	
Presentation package	Developing and modelling information
E-mail	

The ICT tests assess candidates' capability with each of the six applications across the three skills areas. The tests are set in educational contexts relevant to newly-qualified teachers. Candidates are introduced to a scenario and have to complete three tasks related to the scenario that draw on both the six applications and the three skills areas. Candidates' actions in responding to the tasks are tracked as part of the data collection and used within the marking procedure by the custom-built software.

The scenario for the test illustrated is a school's visit to a fictitious stately home, Ardean Hall; all tasks within the test relate to preparation for the visit. The first sample screen (see Figure 7.9, below) shows the desktop as presented in the test. The desktop provides all necessary background information and contains icons representing each of the six applications given above.

Figure 7.9: *ICT Skills Test: desktop*

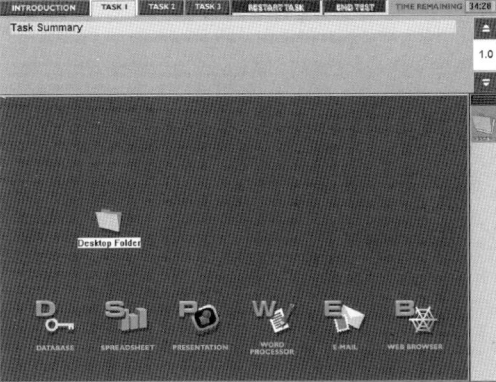

The next three examples (see Figures 7.10, 7.11, 7.12 on page 86) show screens from the three tasks required in order to complete the whole test. These parts of the task involve preparing a handout for use at the visit. The task requires, amongst other things, the finding and use of websites (including one for the DfES website), downloading a picture and amending material for a class handout. Information and instructions are always provided on the top part of the screen.

Figure 7.10: *ICT Skills Test: Chisham School Visit*

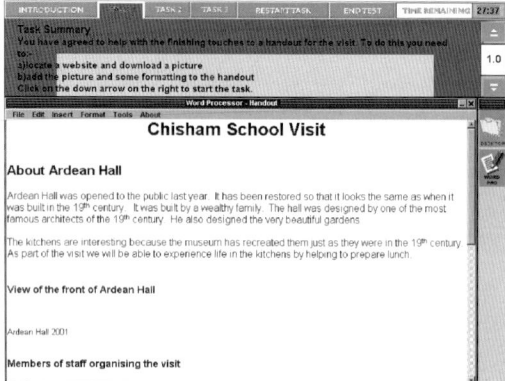

Figure 7.11: *ICT Skills Test: Ardean Hall website*

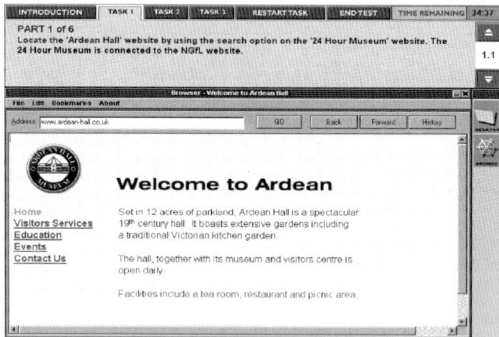

Figure 7.12: *ICT Skills Test: using The Standards Site*

The next example (see Figure 7.13, below) shows an element of the second task, which involves:
- the opening, reading, updating, replying to and sending of e-mails;
- word processing;
- use of a database and a spreadsheet relating to the costs of travelling and visiting the historic house.

All the material used is drawn from a common educational context.

The final example, shown in Figure 7.14, below, relates to stages of developing a presentation for parents around the theme of the school's visit to Ardean Hall. This task requires the use of presentation software; candidates are required to change and update a number of given slides from a presentation. Instructions are given at the top of the page.

Figure 7.13: *ICT Skills Test: e-mail screen shot*

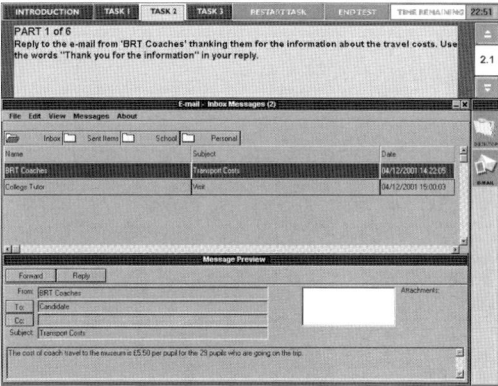

Figure 7.14: *ICT Skills Test: 'Presentation to Parents'*

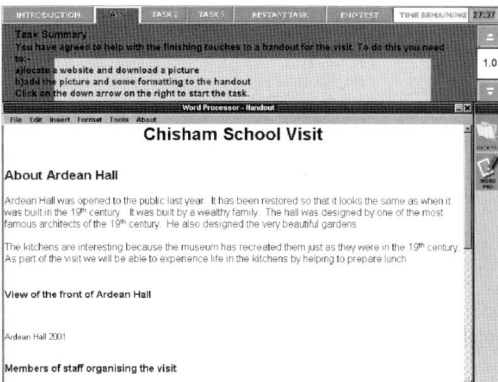

SUPPORT MATERIALS

As already highlighted, the QTS Skills Tests are high stakes tests: all trainee teachers must pass the tests if they are to be qualified to teach. Additionally, the tests are new and are the first computerised national tests to be used in England. Trainee teachers are unlikely to have any experience of this type of test; furthermore, they may not have practised their literacy or numeracy skills in a testing setting for some years. In order to support the candidates, especially during the first two years of operation of the tests, sample materials were produced. In 2000, these were in hard-copy format and included audiotapes enabling candidates to practise their mental arithmetic and spelling; practice tests were also downloadable from the website. In 2001, these were replaced by CD-ROM versions, together with new interactive downloadable practice tests.

Lessons learned

As might be expected in a project of this kind, it was well recognised that there was a significant amount of risk involved. However, the good use made of the detailed project brief, and of effective project management tools such as the risk register, helped to limit known risks and prompted the identification and effective management of new ones. From the outset, TTA took advice from representative groups before developing policy and a range of different tests; this proved very valuable and put TTA in a strong position for meeting the specific needs of individual trainees.

PRESENTING THE TESTS TO THE PUBLIC

One area in which TTA learned a great deal throughout the project's development related to how the Skills Tests were presented in the public arena. As mentioned earlier, the high stakes nature of the tests, and the fact that they were seen as an imposed requirement, caused, perhaps not surprisingly, some hostility and controversy. In particular, a number of ITT providers were initially opposed to the tests and the media took a significant interest. The trainee teachers, therefore, were unsettled; more often than not, they were picking up from the media incorrect information about their position. The project team had to deal effectively with a large volume of telephone enquiries and written correspondence – not only from trainee teachers, but also from parents and Members of Parliament. However, TTA learnt that its robust and fast response to such enquiries was effective and, as expected, the volume of enquiries and the media interest decreased markedly as the test settled down.

The area of policy that prompted the greatest number of complaints and the most concerns was the limiting of the number of attempts at each test to four. This was reported to be causing the candidates to feel under pressure, and after a few months the policy was amended to allow for unlimited attempts. In fact, as the trainee teachers became more familiar with the test requirements and made better use of the support materials, the pressure dissipated. To date, at least 92 per cent of candidates have passed a test within two attempts.

THE TEST CENTRE MODEL

From the outset, the test centre model worked better than expected. However, a number of difficulties surfaced, which had to be overcome: this was not surprising for such an innovative and large-scale project. Some of these problems related to aspects such as the location, staffing, equipping and sustaining of the effective operation of particular test centres; others were centred on the technical aspects of the project. This was where TTA learnt the real value of having contracted a managing agent to cover the work of all the test centres; the agent provided a dedicated helpline for both the centres and the trainee teachers and also provided a resource for troubleshooting difficulties.

LIMITATIONS AND BENEFITS OF THE DELIVERY SYSTEM

The information gleaned from various sources had led TTA to believe that more creative approaches to computerised testing were available than proved to be the case. The project team had to learn quickly to revise their expectations. For example, it was agreed that the testing of literacy should include writing but computerised testing of 'free writing' was not (and is not yet) ready for use on a wide scale.

TTA learnt to recognise the vital importance of ensuring the technical stability of the tests themselves within the delivery system before launching them; the team was also aware of the likely impact of less-than-perfect tests on the candidates.

Everyone anticipated that, in the very early days, there were likely to be difficulties with the delivery of some tests, despite extensive quality assurance testing of the system. When problems arose, much work went into solving them as quickly as possible and learning from them, and the system was soon running smoothly. It has subsequently proved to be very reliable and secure, meeting the requirements for:
• the downloading of a large number of tests;
• all booked tests to be available on demand and at the expected time;
• the essential tracking of all candidate details and results year-on-year.

Despite the early hiccoughs, TTA believes that it has chosen a robust system with a good track record gained over a significant period.

MANAGEMENT OF THE CONTRACTORS

Evidence suggests that projects such as this one often run into problems. These difficulties are often associated with the outside contractors appointed and differing perceptions of the roles of the various parties. However, from the beginning TTA found that by managing this aspect tightly, through working closely with contractors, it learnt the value of developing highly-effective professional relationships in producing a successful outcome. Time was allocated for regular face-to-face meetings throughout the project, first together as an in-house team, and then with the respective contractors. This was time well spent, as it enabled early clarification of the full intent of the project brief and minimised potential misunderstandings of requirements. Even more importantly, perhaps, it enabled all parties to gain a good understanding of each other's ways of working and to see how to use this knowledge to best effect in achieving the project's aim.

Where next?

MAINTAINING AND UPDATING THE TESTS

TTA's original plan included a yearly cycle of updating the content for each of the Skills Test areas in order to include more recent material. This involves at least 10 per cent replenishment. During the first replenishment cycle there are no plans to diverge from the existing arrangements. In the future, however, changes may well take place. For example, as mentioned earlier, the literacy test could include 'free writing', once this can be tested effectively. The development of more creative and innovative material and testing approaches is clearly a possibility in time but, of course, this would need to be considered against the 'fitness for purpose' requirement and would also have to be weighed against value for money.

Finding ways of supporting trainee teachers even more effectively is at the top of TTA's agenda. In particular, TTA will be considering how to make better use of interactivity so that the downloadable support materials are better able to help candidates as they improve and hone their skills in literacy, numeracy and ICT.

IMPROVING ACCESS AND AVAILABLITY

The delivery of the tests via TTA's 50 test centres may well be an area that needs further examination. TTA will look at new and different scenarios to see if better means of access to, and availability of, the Skills Tests may be secured. At present, for example, only final-year trainee teachers are allowed to take the tests. In the longer term, TTA needs to consider opening up the system to other cohorts of trainee teachers and possibly to those who are applying to undertake training. However, there are significant implications for such a move, not the least of which concerns the tracking management problems that would have to be overcome before this could become a reality.

Another area of interest for the future is the notion of offering testing that is truly available 'on demand', anywhere and at any time. However, such a facility begs many questions, which are yet to be answered. The successful operation of such a system, particularly for high stakes tests such as the Skills Tests, would raise significant technical, security, invigilation and business issues.

Conclusion

The Skills Tests have been operational since February 2001; the second cohort of trainee teachers began taking the tests in September 2001; the first full academic year of operation was completed in July 2002. TTA has already begun to consider possible amendments through drawing on the experience and analysis of results to date. Potential developments for the future are being researched and will assist TTA as it further develops large-scale computerised testing. TTA's hope is that it will be able to assist others by sharing its learning and the benefits of its experience.

8 Computer-based assessment of basic and key skills: quality and compliance

Michael Kingdon
Independent adviser, Sutton, Sandy, UK

Introduction

THIS CHAPTER REPORTS ON A SERIES OF RESEARCH STUDIES conducted in January 2002, by QCA and seven awarding bodies, into the delivery of basic and key skills tests for levels 1 (foundation) and 2 (intermediate). It draws on the complete report on the research studies (QCA, 2002a) received by the basic and key skills project board in April 2002.

The report concluded that the basic technologies required to deliver basic and key skills tests online and on-screen to centres had already been established by the awarding bodies that participated in the studies. The findings and experiences gained from the management of the studies were generalised to:

- identify the general models that might be used for the IT-based delivery of basic and key skills – not only at levels 1 and 2, but also at levels 3 (advanced) and 4 (higher);
- develop principles and recommendations for the implementation of online and on-screen testing in the short to medium term (key elements of these included the use by awarding bodies and centres of mixed delivery models, the ability of awarding bodies to select from available technologies, and the need for adequate training of centre staff and the candidates);
- identify issues for consideration in the future accreditation of awarding bodies to deliver the basic and key skills qualifications, and, in future, systems for quality assurance;
- identify the first examples of good and bad practice in the IT-based delivery of basic and key skills tests;
- explore the implications for test quality and compliance policies.

The presentation of the report coincided with the Ministerial decision to implement monthly testing of basic and key skills from April 2002 and weekly testing from

September 2002. Many stakeholders made the assumption that the latter date constituted a target for the implementation of the first ICT-based basic and key skills tests.

Further information on the basic and key skills testing programme may be found on the QCA website (www.qca.org.uk), under the heading 'National Qualifications', and in the *Key Skills Qualifications Specification and Guide* (QCA, 2002b).

The organisation of the January 2002 research studies

The purpose of the research studies was to explore the issues that will be associated with the on-demand, and in some cases on-screen, delivery of basic and key skills tests. The outcomes of the research studies informed the planning of weekly testing of basic and key skills, which was introduced in England in 2002.

The tests are delivered by a large and heterogeneous group of centres, including:
• schools;
• colleges;
• commercial training organisations;
• armed services training establishments;
• employment services centres;
• prisons and other secure training and/or assessment centres;
• professional bodies;
• approved company training schemes.

The following factors pointed to the need for flexible delivery arrangements:
• the differing needs and resources of the awarding bodies, their centres and candidates;
• the nature of the tests: basic and key skills tests at levels 1 and 2 use multiple-choice items, whilst questions for levels 3 and 4 make use of a wider variety of question forms and are closer in format to traditional examination and national curriculum models;
• whilst the use of ICT-based assessment was assumed to be a key feature in the delivery of tests to candidates in some types of centre, it is understood that some awarding bodies and centres will continue to use paper-based tests.

QCA asked participating awarding bodies to trial methods of delivering on-demand tests to their centres in January 2002; if they already had appropriate systems, they were asked to trial on-screen presentation as well. All awarding bodies that wished to be involved had to agree to deliver at least one test, on demand, to a sample of their centres: most chose to use tests for all three of the basic and key skills subjects, and at both levels 1 and 2.

As the tests used in the research studies were timetabled for a week after the scheduled January test window, special sets of level 1 and 2 tests were constructed for all three skill areas: Communication/Adult Literacy, Application of Number/ Numeracy and IT. With one exception, these tests were developed to the same specifications as the January mainstream tests, were drawn from the same item banks and contained the same numbers of items (40). The exception related to Application of Number papers – where, to avoid any issues with different sizes of monitor screens, questions requiring measurement were replaced with estimation questions.

The research studies departed from the approaches used in the scheduled basic and key skills tests in two ways. First, the participating awarding bodies were asked to deliver results to centres within seven to 10 working days – a target that has been set for some later scheduled tests. Secondly, as several of the on-screen models had the potential to produce immediate feedback of results to centres and candidates, the use of pre-set pass marks for each test was explored, using the available psychometric data for the selected items. The pre-set pass marks were not used to make the awards, but the test results from the on-screen systems were monitored for evidence to confirm or question the pre-set pass marks.

The tests were scheduled to take place during the last week of January. They were provided to the awarding bodies in a number of electronic formats, and as camera-ready copy (CRC). In anticipation of some awarding bodies using on-screen delivery, the tests were structured with one item (question) per page and all scenario items (items that were grouped into sets around common stimulus material) repeated the stimulus material for each item.

Unusually for a trial test for a recognised qualification, success in the tests led to a recognised pass, and the results were subsumed into those for the scheduled January test window.

On-demand systems

Three awarding bodies – EMTA Awards Limited (EAL), London Chamber of Commerce and Industry (LCCI) and Oxford, Cambridge and Royal Society of Arts (OCR) – opted to take part by providing the tests online to their participating centres. In anticipation of on-demand test delivery, all three awarding bodies used encrypted internet systems to deliver the tests to centres. The centres were required to download and print out the tests for presentation to candidates. Candidates' responses were recorded using optical mark reader (OMR) or optical character recognition (OCR) forms. These forms were read by the awarding bodies, and results were returned within seven to 10 days. All centres were provided with sealed copies of the test papers, in case the electronic delivery methods should fail. In one case, a compact disk (CD) was also used as back-up.

COMMENTS ON THE ON-DEMAND DELIVERY SYSTEMS

The three research studies demonstrated that it is possible to deliver tests electronically and on-demand to centres and that it would also be possible to reduce the time between pupil registration and test delivery to a matter of days. Two issues have been identified that will need to form part of the next round of approvals to conduct basic and key skills testing. First, the awarding bodies will need to satisfy themselves, their centres, candidates and the regulator (QCA) about the technical efficiency – specifically the security and technical reliability – of the methods used to deliver the tests to centres electronically and on-demand. They will also need to decide whether further contingent back-ups will be needed to ensure test delivery at the correct time and using the method expected by the centres. Secondly, the awarding bodies and regulator will need assurance concerning the security of the downloading, printing and administration procedures in the centres that choose the on-demand systems.

On-demand on-screen systems

Four awarding bodies – the Assessment and Qualifications Alliance (AQA), City and Guilds, Edexcel and the Institute of the Motor Industry (IMI) – agreed to provide on-demand and on-screen methods of delivering tests to their centres. The systems developed by two of the awarding bodies were broadly similar in design and management. Both involved the use of:
• online delivery of tests;
• online registration of candidates for the tests;
• use of an 'invigilator's terminal' to manage and monitor the candidates taking the tests;
• on-screen presentation of test items and recording of results;
• online reporting of results to the awarding bodies.

One system had been developed for other on-screen testing projects and was adapted to meet the needs of the study. This system has the capability to provide immediate results and profiles to candidates through the use of the invigilator's terminal in each centre. Staff in the other awarding body were developing similar functions for their system.

The system used by a third awarding body was, again, an adaptation of systems already in use for other on-demand, on-screen test purposes. Although it used different technical systems, its functionality closely paralleled that used by one of the two awarding bodies reported above. The one important difference was that the initial delivery of the tests to the centres was by CD.

The final awarding body's system for on-screen test delivery differed from the other three in a number of important respects:

• It did not involve the use of an invigilator's terminal and staff in the centres had to conduct the log-on procedure for each candidate.

• Candidates remained online to the awarding body during the tests, and questions were handed down individually. Although this approach to on-screen testing could provide flexibility in the items – and tests – delivered to individual candidates, the total numbers of centres and candidates that can be supported at the same time are finite.

INITIAL COMMENTS ON THE FOUR ONLINE ON-SCREEN SYSTEMS
All four systems had adapted the test items successfully. There were, of course, variations in the quality and style with which this was done. Three were of a high technical quality and made use of colour; the fourth was less sophisticated and used a black-on-white format.

The need for candidates to scroll up and down the screen in order to see a whole question was not considered to be good practice.

All four systems provided a sample test, which candidates could use to familiarise themselves with the test procedures: some sample tests were freestanding and could be used in advance of the test; others were integral parts of the test introduction.

In all four cases, candidates were able to see a 'navigation bar' showing which questions they had answered. While all the candidates had the ability to select their own order of questions, some of those using the full online system found this to be a slow process.

No evidence was found to suggest that the pre-set pass marks had been incorrectly determined and all seven awarding bodies used them to make their awards. The appropriateness of the pass marks was confirmed by an Angoff procedure, which is the most commonly used procedure for setting pass marks for a broad range of certification examinations. The Angoff procedure was organised by AQA as part of its contribution to the overall work. Looking forward, it would appear likely that pre-set pass marks and instant feedback of results to centres and candidates will become part of some of the online on-screen models used to deliver basic and key skills tests in the future.

It was clear from feedback from the trial centres and candidates that centres associated the provision of a profile of results, which the on-screen models were able to provide (as opposed to a simple pass/fail result), with increased validity. The production of a profile in turn raises issues about the actions that could follow when a level 1 candidate *just* fails a test, especially if his or her performance is heterogeneous. In such a case, is a complete resit the best way forward for the candidate, or should other courses of action be considered?

New delivery models

LEVELS 1 AND 2
Three models have been identified as possible ways of managing the delivery of weekly testing at levels 1 and 2.

Model 1
Model 1 is a fully electronic version, with:
- tests delivered to centres online;
- tests presented to candidates on-screen;
- responses being recorded via the screen;
- responses submitted to the awarding body online;
- results notified by the awarding body online.

Model 1 has the potential to deliver immediate results for level 1 and 2 candidates. Centres may therefore wish to use this model as a diagnostic and formative tool at level 1. It is likely to be a low-volume model in the immediate future but has the potential to become a high-volume model, given improved technology.

Model 2
Model 2 is a part-electronic version, with:
- tests being delivered to centres online;

- tests presented to candidates on-screen or printed out onto paper;
- responses being recorded on computer readable forms (using OMR, OCR or intelligent character recognition [ICR] technology);
- responses submitted to the awarding body by post;
- results notified by the awarding body online within seven to 10 working days.

Model 2 uses electronic systems to deliver tests to centres and candidates at short notice. With pre-specification of pass marks, test results could be collected, processed and reported by an awarding body in seven to 10 working days – the target that has been set for basic and key skills reporting.

Model 3

Model 3 is the 'traditional examination' model and involves:
- tests being delivered to centres through the post or by courier;
- tests presented to candidates on paper;
- responses being recorded on computer readable forms (OMR/OCR);
- responses submitted to the awarding body by post;
- *post hoc* awards and results notified by the awarding body in approximately 20 to 30 working days.

Until Model 1 and the use of pre-set pass marks become the standard for levels 1 and 2, Model 3 will continue to be the high-volume model. It is also likely to remain the default model for smaller awarding bodies.

From discussion with the awarding bodies before and during the research studies, it appears that they may wish to offer a menu of delivery models, in order to meet a variety of centre needs. There will be a 'mixed economy' of delivery models and centres can expect to exercise choice between different models for the foreseeable future.

LEVELS 3 AND 4

The experience of conducting the research studies has also pointed the way forward for levels 3 and 4. To achieve the required speed of turnaround of the results it was assumed that, except for very small-volume models, *images* of candidates' answers would be marked and moderated in preference to candidates' actual *papers*. Existing test models that already make use of marking from images of candidates answers were reviewed; selections suitable for different test volumes and frequencies are proposed.

Model 1

Model 1 is a fully electronic version, with:
- tests being delivered to centres online;
- tests presented to candidates on-screen;
- candidates keying their responses directly into their computer;
- responses submitted to the marker online, perhaps by way of the awarding body's server;
- marking and moderation being conducted using the electronic image produced by the candidate;
- results notified by the awarding body online and potentially on-return.

Model 1 is assumed to be a low-volume model – at least in the early years – as it depends on candidates being willing to type their responses directly into a computer. It has the potential to be a large-volume model.

Model 2

Model 2 uses a part-electronic system to deliver the test to the candidate, who responds on paper. Thereafter this model follows the traditional examination model, with:

- tests being delivered to centres online;
- tests presented to candidates on-screen;
- candidates writing their answers on answer scripts;
- scripts submitted to the marker by mail;
- marking and moderation being conducted using candidates' answer scripts by markers working at the awarding bodies' offices;
- results notified by the awarding body online within seven to 10 working days.

Model 2 contrasts with Model 4 (below) by using electronic systems to support and speed the beginning of the testing process, rather than the end. Model 2 uses electronic systems to deliver the tests, whereas Model 4 uses them to speed the marking.

Model 3

Model 3 is the traditional examination model that uses:

- tests delivered to centres through the post or by courier;
- tests presented to candidates on paper;
- candidates writing their answers on answer scripts;
- scripts submitted to the marker by mail;
- marking and moderation being conducted using candidates' answer scripts;
- results notified by the awarding body online within 40 working days.

Model 3, like its equivalent for levels 1 and 2, will remain the high-volume model until the potential of Models 1 and 4 is achieved. Again, it will remain the default model for some awarding bodies.

Model 4

If the traditional examination model is likely to prove too slow, a candidate's answer script could be imaged and computer-based methods of marking could be used thereafter. The key features of Model 4 are as follows:

- tests delivered to centres through the post or by courier;
- tests presented to candidates on paper;
- candidates writing their answers on answer scripts;
- scripts imaged and decollated for imaging;
- images sent electronically to the marker, with some sections of the answers marked electronically using OCR;
- electronic communications between the moderator and marker;
- results notified by the awarding body online within – say – 20 to 25 working days.

Although the introduction of IT-based systems is expected to be slower for levels above level 2, again centres can expect to have a choice of models in the short and medium term.

Whither the delivery of basic and key skills tests?

Following the research studies and the thinking about delivery models that has followed them, four issues have come to the fore; these issues, and the challenges that they present, are discussed below.

CHANGES TO THE MANAGEMENT OF MARKERS

The development of online on-screen models for testing at levels 3 and 4 has highlighted the increasing need for a permanently available core of markers, each with online access to central marking systems. The issue of test item resources and the need to report more quickly are also making demands on the roles and working practices of the moderators, who will be used to supervise markers and to assure the quality of their marking.

At levels 3 and 4, were the form of the test to be closer to traditional examinations, there would be an important additional role for moderators, especially in the early stages of implementation of the new delivery models. Until well-calibrated questions become available in sufficient quantities, moderators could make a greater contribution to awards for the low-volume, online on-screen models.

The project staff are aware that similar development of the roles and working practices of markers and moderator is taking place elsewhere in QCA. This work will be monitored for its potential contribution to the basic and key skills projects.

ON-DEMAND DELIVERY

The ultimate aim of the work reported in this chapter is the development of on-demand test delivery, with candidates being able to take the tests at times that are convenient to them – registration periods being kept to a minimum and results being reported rapidly. At present, however, there are two factors indicating that true on-demand delivery of the basic and key skills tests remains a vision for implementation in the middle- to long-term future.

First, the delivery technologies have currently outstripped the supply of good test items and many issues about item quality remain to be addressed. The main thrust of the basic and key skills programme is therefore focusing on the provision of sufficient quantities of good test items to support weekly test delivery. Secondly, the early versions of the delivery technologies currently being developed by the awarding bodies have yet to prove their technical reliability and acceptability to candidates and centres. The introduction of IT-based delivery systems and the concept of on-demand delivery raise fundamental questions about the regulation of basic and key skills testing – and, by implication, the future delivery of other national qualifications.

ITEM AND TEST COMPARABILITY

The timetable for the implementation of the basic and key skills tests precludes prior investigations to determine whether the presentation of tests on-screen will change significantly the psychometric properties of the test items. However, similar issues might equally be raised about the different ways in which the participating awarding bodies present the same questions – their differing item layouts, quality of design and use of colour – and whether these also make items easier or more difficult. Further, it has always been part of the basic and key skills philosophy that awarding bodies could 'contextualise' items to meet the needs of specialist candidatures, although this option has not so far been implemented.

These issues of inter-agency test comparability have not been raised before because the tests have all been produced to a single format and approved by QCA. For the awarding bodies, test production has, broadly speaking, been a badging and distribution exercise. Issues of test item efficiency and test comparability over time have been addressed at inter-agency award meetings, which QCA representatives attend.

Many professionals who work with the current basic and key skills tests believe that changes to the layout of test items results in changes to the psychometric properties of the items. These concerns were compounded in the research studies by the production of the pre-award test pass marks. While the research studies were of too small a scale for the pre-set pass marks to be questioned, this issue – and the questions used – will be kept under review during the early months of the weekly testing programme.

Important as these issues are, in the short term they will be less important that some of the practical issues that awarding bodies and centres will face when implementing the online on-screen delivery models for basic and key skills tests.

CHANGES TO REGULATION AND COMPLIANCE PROCESSES

The research studies have shown the importance of training for centre personnel, not only those who will be concerned with the technical aspects of test delivery but also those who will administer the test. The studies have emphasised the need for both groups of personnel to work together, within the guidance and support structures that the awarding bodies provide.

To emphasise the importance of the training and in-centre working, it may be necessary to make the completion of training and the development of in-centre systems – perhaps even their formal certification – a condition for the centre to use particular delivery models.

As indicated above, the findings of the research studies will have implications for the regulation of the models. As part of its contribution to this work, the project team is identifying the general issues that will need to be addressed and those that relate to the individual test models. The first issue here is where in the hierarchy of the regulator (QCA), the regulated (awarding body), and the centres decisions should be made about:

• the models that are to be used for delivery of a particular level and subject;
• the technical requirements that should be specified for the delivery of each model;
• the levels of technical reliability that are essential for the delivery of each model.

Some might argue that all the above issues are the responsibility of the regulator; others may reason that they should be left to the awarding body once general approval to deliver the qualification is granted. It can also be reasoned that, wherever the administrative responsibility is eventually placed, it will be market forces that determine which models are used, and by whom.

Regulators are always likely to be required to take responsibility for quality assurance, one aspect of which is the identification and dissemination of good practice. The research studies revealed some features that individual awarding bodies are using, which, in the author's view, should become part of all awarding body IT-

based delivery systems. Examples include:
- the disabling of standard PC functions that might assist candidates in responding to items or impugn the integrity or security of the tests;
- the use of invigilators' terminals to manage test receipt, test delivery to candidates, test monitoring, results collection, back-ups and test submission processes;
- sample tests, to enable candidates to become familiar with test presentation processes, and training to assist candidates with test-answering strategies.

Similarly, there are features seen during the research studies that should be avoided in future, where possible:
- lengthy design work by QCA and awarding body personnel to prepare the tests for online distribution and on-screen presentation;
- lengthy introductions to the tests and reiterations of the test regulations;
- the need to scroll and/or shift screens in order for candidates to see all the parts of a question;
- excessive waiting times as questions are downloaded;
- corruption of the test item layouts, diagrams and special fonts caused by electronic transmission systems.

These lists will lengthen as the research study reports are reviewed.

Some issues are less clear-cut. There are ongoing discussions concerning:
- whether there should be a standard system to deliver tests to centres, or whether awarding bodies should be allowed to develop their own, to a general specification;
- the extent to which the test-authoring process needs to be developed to meet the needs of online and on-screen test systems;
- what form of preparation should be provided for candidates about to take on-screen tests;
- extensions to the use of predetermined pass marks;
- the nature of the contingent arrangements that will be needed to support online on-screen tests at awarding body and centre levels;
- which of the methods of delivering the tests to centres during the research studies proved to be most successful.

Conclusion: continuing research

The development of IT-based delivery of basic and key skills tests is being taken forward by a further series of research studies. This second series of studies aims to facilitate the development work being undertaken by the awarding bodies.

At the time of writing, four awarding bodies have indicated that they are working towards the implementation of IT-based delivery systems for basic and key skills tests, levels 1 and 2, towards the end of 2002. A second group have reported their intentions to develop such systems for implementation later in the academic year, 2002–2003. Only one awarding body that is currently accredited to deliver the tests has reported that it does *not* have plans to develop an IT-based delivery system. Nevertheless, as mentioned earlier, it is anticipated that a 'mixed economy' of both paper-based and computer-based tests will continue for the foreseeable future.

The research projects will monitor the development work of the awarding bodies and assist with the resolution of any issues that are outside their direct control. The studies will also identify the issues that will need to be considered in future accreditation and quality assurance systems, informing QCA's implementation of IT-based delivery methods for other national qualifications.

Finally, on a practical level, the second series of research studies will provide all those involved with opportunities to share problems – and hopefully solutions – with QCA as regulator, other regulators and one another.

PART III

The Curricular Effects of Assessment

Overview

Martin Ripley

Qualifications and Curriculum Authority (QCA), London, UK

This final part of *Whither Assessment?* juxtaposes chapters on the effects that technology can have on learning and assessment for learning, and on the extent to which computer-delivered assessments can provide a platform for better tests.

As explained in the Preface, the 'Whither Assessment?' seminar, on which this book is based, was designed to explore two themes in the future of assessment: the application of technology to educational assessment and 'assessment for learning'. The purpose of Part III of the book is to examine the roles of assessment in shaping and directing learning and to suggest that improvements in the ways in which we observe, evaluate and assess our students can rewrite our assumptions about how students learn and monitor their own progress. It is also interesting to note that technology and assessment for learning are in many ways poised to play a major role in education during the next decade.

Technology provides the opportunity and challenge for us to rethink *what we value* in education and how we *assess* what we value. Perhaps no-one expresses these notions as profoundly as Stephen Heppell, author of Chapter 9. This chapter, redolent with radicalism and vision, asks the reader to consider why we use traditional forms of assessment to constrain and control students' work and learning. Extending themes explored in Part II of this book, Stephen Heppell asks us to consider why our assessment systems have changed so little and why, through our concern to standardise and systematise assessment, we have squeezed out of our students so much of their potential to demonstrate their capabilities. In our desire to standardise, have we effectively placed a ceiling on student performance? In our desire and need to standardise and measure learning on a national basis, have we restricted our students to a traditional set of assessment practices?

Stephen Heppell challenges us, as educators and assessors, to consider whether we are implementing systems designed to lead students to convey their learning only through the lenses worn in traditional forms of assessment. Similarly, the two chapters on assessment for learning, Chapters 10 and 11, lead us to rethink the ways in which we, as teachers, have used assessment in the classroom, the extent to which we provide students with tools to control their own learning, and how we use our own limited vision to make decisions about students' understanding.

Gordon Stobart, in Chapter 10, sets out the case for assessment for learning. 'Using assessment to improve learning: intentions, feedback and motivation' provides us with a clear understanding of how classroom practices and the teacher's assessment of (and relationship with) students affect learning. With echoes of Stephen Heppell's chapter (the reader might wonder whether Stephen Heppell and Gordon Stobart went to the same primary school), Gordon Stobart argues the case for the students excluded and demotivated by traditional assessment rituals and routines.

In Chapter 11, Christine Harrison and Sue Swaffield provide us with one of the first published articles on research undertaken from King's College London in assessment for learning. The chapter takes as its starting point the publications of Paul Black and Dylan Wiliam, including *Inside the Black Box* (Black and Wiliam, 1998b). It gives us a glimpse of the potential power of the Black and Wiliam message and provides compelling evidence that assessment for learning works. In a slightly ironic twist, assessment for learning, the authors claim, can even improve school performance as measured by traditional forms of assessment. The chapter links well with Part I of this book, particularly the chapters by Shirley Clarke and Ronald Gallimore and James Stigler.

The final chapter in the book, Chapter 12, has been written by two colleagues who have worked with QCA in designing tests that have demonstrated to the world the feasibility of building better tests, through the World Class Tests project. By using the computer to present students with problems to solve, in a dynamic and motivating environment, Hugh Burkhardt, Daniel Pead and their colleagues at the Mathematics Assessment Resource Service (MARS), based at the Universities of Durham and Nottingham, have, I think, demonstrated that the worlds envisaged by Stephen Heppell and others are attainable, even if as policymakers we feel unable to embrace the entire Heppell vision. Hugh Burkhardt and Daniel Pead offer the reader a rationale and analysis of some of the problem solving activities that appear in the World Class Tests.

---

9 Assessment and new technology: new straitjackets or new opportunities?

Stephen Heppell
Ultralab, Anglia Polytechnic University, Chelmsford, UK

Introduction

TECHNOLOGY EXCITES CHILDREN and has been applied in industrial, military and commercial settings to massive advantage. This chapter examines ways in which children can, when offered technological tools and creative opportunities, demonstrate unexpected skills and capabilities.

Industry has been quick to see the commercial potential of technology and moves rapidly to find economic uses for the latest technological developments. But when we teach our children and when we assess them, we demonstrate contrasting habits. We value the educational approaches, the assessments and the standards of former generations. We withhold from our children the opportunities that technology provides for an expansion of the assessment process. We withhold from them the opportunity to be creative with new technology and to celebrate the progression of their new capabilities.

This chapter proposes that children are capable of achieving much, much more than our schools and assessment systems allow them to. Technology might, if applied to the assessment process, offer opportunities to change this. However, neither the potential of technology nor the willingness of our educators to embrace it are clear as yet. Several examples of work and projects that demonstrate this potential are described in this chapter; many more such ambitious explorations are needed if the new opportunities presented by technology are not to be wasted. Such explorations will enable us to gauge our willingness as educators to drop the constraints we place on our children when we ask them to show us what they know and can do.

The influence of past technologies on assessment

Before we get too exercised about the revolutionary impact that ICT might have on assessment, it is instructive to reflect on the extent to which our current assessment techniques have been distorted by the technologies of the past. The two examples that follow illustrate this well.

'WIRED' BUT HAMSTRUNG

A second generation of students is now enjoying mastery of the word processor, with all its agility and opportunities to revise or refine text. This ubiquitous machine, in various guises and brands, has been found in classrooms since the beginning of the 1980s. However, our second 'wired' generation is very rarely offered a chance to demonstrate its new literacy and creativity using the word processor in an assessment setting. Students restricted once again to pen and paper must rely, as many moderators have found, on a patchwork of arrows, insertions and crossings out. The older technologies reveal themselves to be poor vehicles for the students' new creativity and literacy.

SEEN BUT NOT HEARD

Another example of distortion is the way past technologies drove oracy out of our schools. Every parent, employer, teacher and student will testify to the importance of the spoken word in communicating, discussing, collaborating and demonstrating understanding. Yet, until we reach the giddy heights of a doctorate, with its interrogative *viva*, oracy is almost entirely absent from our assessment experience. Why is this? Some years ago, our technology began to speed up some aspects of the assessment process. We realised, however, that it offered no solution to the need for rapid moderation of students' oral work. We had no tools for rapid indexing or for skimming speech and no way of analysing spoken contributions. Because the tools were non-existent, we conveniently forgot that the thing we were finding impossible to moderate was fundamentally important. Probably, we should have trusted teachers more and taken more account of their judgement. After all, countless school reports had already reflected, 'If only her written work were as good as her spoken contribution, she would be top of the class ...'

The challenge of difference

The above examples show that there is a mismatch between the assessments that we *want* to make available in schools and the limitations that the older technologies – pens, optical mark readers (OMR) and the like – impose on us. Mercifully, we now have tools for dealing effectively with spoken contributions. Indeed, for many years our national security agencies have been turning telephone calls into text with considerable accuracy, which begs the question, 'Why we have been so slow to harness the same well-tested commercially available technologies for assessment purposes?'

MISLEADING 'DIFFERENCE'

Part of the answer to that conundrum lies in the need of policymakers and politicians to demonstrate that they have 'made a difference', trapping us in the unambitious quicksand of criterion referencing. 'We spent more and – look, things are better!' is the clear message that re-elects political parties. Sadly, given the pace of change of new technology and the speed with which students' sense of entitlement accelerates alongside it, the best we know that we will be able to offer is, 'We spent more and look – things are different! And here is our *evidence* to show that *different is better!*' This claim will win less hearts and minds at the ballot box, unless the evidence that 'different is better' is clearly presented, persuasive and available in the public domain.

DIFFERENCE UNRECOGNISED

One of many sorrows about the impact of much current assessment is that students' best work, the work that results from focus and intense application, is produced for the assessment process, yet is rarely seen or celebrated by any audience other than examiners and moderators. In a recent exploration of creativity (part of a confidential national education policy consultancy for a Pacific rim nation), students were asked about the piece of work that they were most proud of having produced. Over three-quarters reported that the work was produced as a direct assessment output. The supplementary questions, 'Where is that work now?' and 'Did your parents see that work?' were, largely, met with 'Don't know' and 'No' respectively. This is not only tragic for the individuals involved; it also represents a substantial missed opportunity for the nation. If we are to win hearts and minds in moving education forward ambitiously, this crucial evidence of excellence has a key role in persuading nations that students' work, even where it is very *different* from what went before, is showing a real improvement.

CELEBRATING DIFFERENCE

'*Different*' is inevitable. New technology advances apace and this, of course, is well documented. Computers are designed with computers; the better they are, the faster we can use them to design even more sophisticated ones. Computers, seen or unseen, are everyday tools for us all, but their value in learning is as *tools* for creativity and learning, rather than as *machines* to 'deliver' the curriculum.

These tools, in our children's hands, are forever pushing the envelope of expertise that previous technologies excluded them from. For example, children can now:
- analyse, compose and perform music before acquiring any ability to play an instrument;
- shoot, edit and stream digital video without any support from media courses;
- produce architectural fly-throughs of incredible buildings without any drafting or 2-D skills;
- make stop-frame animations with plasticine models;
- edit and finesse their poetry;
- explore surfaces on their visual calculators;
- swap ideas with scientists online about volcanic activity;
- follow webcam images of ospreys hatching;
- track weather by live satellite images;
- control the robots they have built themselves …

… and generally push at the boundaries of what might be possible, indeed what *was* formerly possible, for people of *any* age, let alone school-age students.

Little of this was easily achieved in the school classroom 10 years ago, although the many projects emanating from Ultralab during the 1990s offered clear enough indicators of what might be possible in the future. The challenge here is to criterion referencing. So often the cry of the teacher, 'That work is better than my degree exhibition piece!' reflects a substantial step-change in both the age at which a creative act can be enjoyed and the quality of the tools supporting that creativity.

STUNTING DIFFERENCE

Unfortunately, this extraordinary potential for progress comes at a time when we are wedded to an assessment model that satisfies us if students attempt the same activities as did their predecessors, but with a little more success. In an age of rapid technological progress, this fatally masks rapidly falling standards and stultifies ambition. On the one hand, new technology supports children's ability to make new leaps of imagination and creativity. In fact, imagination and creativity are sometimes excluded under the feeble pretext that 'We didn't do it like that before'. The result is that schools habitually confiscate or deny new technology – removing everything, from a ballpoint pen ('It will spoil your handwriting') to a mobile phone ('Disruptive!') Teachers report that the best creativity they observe is in the non-curriculum space of lunchtime clubs or out-of-school activities. We have failed to respond within the curriculum and its assessment process to these new opportunities for creativity. The new tools that students should be able to harness for their learning would deliver real productivity, but we have failed to respond to this challenge because we have also failed to set rapidly-rising standards.

Surely we know that students can write better with a word processor? It offers them the opportunity to refine, revisit, draft, finesse and error-check their work. They can take countless risks with their work without the penalty of longhand copying. Word processors bring them new strategies for creative writing – again, strategies that were once the domain of authors, not schoolchildren. Using word processors as tools, students produce more and better work than their earlier peers, and this has been well documented since the 1980s (Johnston, Cox and Rhodes, 1989).

So, 30 years after the first word processors appeared in our classrooms, have we responded by setting much more ambitious targets for children's writing performance? Of course not! We simply exclude the word processor from the examination room under the pretext that it won't allow us to compare their ambitious work with the pen-written output of a previous age. Thus we stunt our children's development, robbing them of both opportunity and ambition. Or worse, we capture the productivity of the computer only for the convenience of our own assessment administration. Wouldn't it be good if the computer could mark our assessments for us? Bluntly, no! In a world where new technology is limited by supply and cost it would be such a wasted opportunity. However, it would be good if the new things that students do with computers might be acknowledged by the ambition and creativity of the targets we set them.

Entitled to communicate

To attempt to face down the constancy of change, the certainty of uncertainty, with the leaden yardstick of past history is palpably silly. Whilst we can take the phone or the word processor out of children's hands we cannot take the accompanying sense of entitlement out of their heads. A major impact of new technology has been the rapidity with which our attitudes change. Ultralab drove the national rebranding of IT (the sterile 'information technology' label) into ICT, where the added 'C' stood for '*and communications*'. New technologies are essentially communication tools: the visual spreadsheets of the 1970s, the desktop publishing of the 1980s, the worldwide web of the 1990s and the computer 'pocketability' of the new millennium have all been communication revolutions. Incidentally, it is interesting to reflect on the extent to which these four massive revolutions have impacted so far on the assessment process: very little. But this revolution in communication has brought with it a sense of *entitlement*, that we should all have a voice in the communication age. We are entitled to communicate with others.

The effects of this entitlement to communicate can be seen in many sectors. For example, people under the age of 35 are falling out of representative democracy all around the world with the cry, 'Why won't our government *listen* to us?!' A sense of entitlement to communicate carries with it a sense of audience and of being an audience for others. The symmetry of communication (essentially a two-way act) has been a difficult concept to embrace. But even those who have had difficulty with it have now begun to realise that without this two-way conduit we lock people out, deny their new sense that technology will give them a voice and role, and generate dissatisfaction, alienation or anomie.

ULTRALAB PROJECTS

A major Ultralab project with the British Broadcasting Corporation (BBC) started in 2002; it finally empowers students to make, broadcast and stream their own programmes, *by* children *for* children. They do this using a variety of broadcasting opportunities including digital terrestrial channels and large screens at football stadiums (BBC/Ultralab, 2001).

In 1996, in another research project at Ultralab, Stan Owers surveyed over 3,000 A level students in order to build a picture of their views of the curriculum, its creativity, relevance, interest and more (Owers, 2002b). Some of the data produced was unsurprising: students interested in a subject tended to be studying it, for example. However, some deeply disturbing trends emerged too. Much of the blame for these trends must be laid at the door of an assessment system that values product over process and that has failed to recognise the changing tide of students' expectations in the age of ICT. For example, the question 'How creative does the curriculum allow you to be in mathematics?' prompted a predictably dismal response from those who had *rejected* mathematics as an A level specialism. But it also brought an almost identical overlaid graph of responses from those who had *chosen* mathematics as an A level option (Owers, 2002a; see also www.ultralab.ac.uk/people/stan_owers). We should be dismayed by this. What had changed, of course, was not the curriculum (indeed the lack of change may be a substantial part of the problem), but the students' new expectations that their learning world might be a creative world too.

Repeating the survey in 2002, again with over 3,000 students, Owers and Constable found that in some ways the situation has declined further. However, there are projects, as described below, which aim to supplement the curriculum with positive creative experiences and to inject the curriculum itself with more opportunities for communication and the use of ICT.

Ultralab summer school

Ultralab runs an annual summer school. Each year, a group of around 100 students are given tough tasks that recent changes in technology have made cheaply accessible to school-age students. Their tasks are phrased in an open-ended way, and they spend a relatively small amount of time in the lab being introduced to both task and technology.

In the summer of 2001, for example, students were confronted with a challenge to produce a 'framed' artwork, which would be shown at the Victoria and Albert museum (V&A), if good enough. The artwork was to be executed not in watercolour or acrylic, but in video and sound. The simple rules include included a requirement to incorporate the artists' names as some form of 'signature' and a limit of two minutes for what was to be a 'looping' collage of images and sound.

Each of the 100 students was given a unique word, for example: 'Dazed', 'Smoothly', 'Tragedy'. Each group of four students rejected three of the given words and adopted one as their theme for this tough collaborative challenge. Only an hour and a half was set aside to introduce the task, the software (iMovie), the computers (iMacs), the cameras (handheld Canon DVs) and to introduce the intended display area in the V&A. Staff and parents were under strict guidance to support the summer schoolers by driving them around and helping with other logistic support, but not to intervene in the production or creative processes. The students were left in no doubt that their work needed to be 'good enough' to be shown at the V&A; they also had the ambitious outcomes of previous, very different, summer schools to help set a goal for their ambitions.

After the summer, and after spending varied amounts of time, typically spread across parts of a week, the students came together to show the fruits of their labour. Each year, the students demonstrate an ambition beyond the expectations of school and curriculum. The teachers are a key part of the process that sets the annual tasks, but in the first year one commented:

> *This has been like an epiphany to me; I had literally no idea of the quality of work that these children might be able to produce. It has changed my whole view of what we teach and what we should teach.*

The 2001 'video collage' group produced work that met the quality standards of the V&A and was previewed to an ecstatic audience. Interestingly, a parent confided at the end of the preview that his own film and media degree final piece had been eclipsed by the work that he had just witnessed from these students, most of whom were only 12 years old.

LESSONS LEARNED

This annual feast of creativity confirms several key lessons for assessment. Firstly, it is clear that the entirely new tasks set annually do not map easily, if indeed at all, onto any pretence of criterion referencing. There is not even an existing genre to pastiche; this is entirely new work, yet technology has allowed the summer school students into the domain of experts very early in their learning lives. It is also clear that the teachers – who are effectively action researchers during the exercise – can make clear and valid judgements about quality to the extent of being clear about what is 'good enough'. Beyond that, however, the key feedback from students reporting their processes (for example in the formal interview and 'crit' that is a part of their V&A show) is critical to injecting any granularity of judgement beyond that 'good enough' hurdle. The product in every case was engaging, but the reported processes offered a fresh perspective, often stunning, always moving our understanding forwards.

Describing the construction of the final pieces enabled the deconstruction and critiquing to be a much more subtle affair. Finally, the clear sense of impending audience served not only as a prime motivator, but was a useful adjunct to the learning process.

Looking at key stage 3 ICT assessment

In the light of all this, it is not unreasonable to ask 'Whither assessment?' A ground-breaking QCA–Ultralab project seeks to explore how some of these lessons might inform the process of assessment. Approaching the task of key stage 3 ICT assessment, the project proposes three steps.

STEP ONE: MAPPING

The first step is a mapping, by the student, of what their starting points are. At key stage 3, students have brought a wide and welcome diversity of experience into their secondary schools. Standards are not about standardisation and helping each learner to map the 'beginning of the key stage 3 journey' is a necessary first step.

STEP TWO: MILESTONES

The second step sees the student posting milestones onto a common website to mark what they consider to be pivotal or significant moments in their work. These milestones might be images, video, sounds, speech or text; each is 'annotated' – initially by the student but subsequently by peers, teachers, even moderators – using a device that effectively allows 'margin notes' on the webpage. A maximum of six milestones is anticipated at this early stage, but the project is highly iterative and doubtless feedback from students and their teachers will inform all the research, including this maximum.

STEP THREE: 'EVIVA'

The final step sees students and their teachers concluding that a sufficient 'distance' has been travelled from the initial starting point to be worthy of credit. At that point, students nominate a time and place and prepare themselves for a telephone call. That call, using text-to-speech technology, poses a series of questions for the student to defend, perhaps in the manner of a 'crit' or *viva*; indeed, we are calling this process the *eViva*. As with any answerphone, the student can re-record responses to each question at any time. Crucially, the questions posed are themselves selected from a list by the student at the initial stage, with feedback advice about the portfolio of questions selected. In this way, the student is already encouraged towards meta-level reflection about their learning through an awareness of the questions to be defended against at the end. The telephone makes an interesting conduit, because sophisticated voice-to-text technology can turn the student's spoken words into text for moderation. A fundamental design intention of this new assessment strategy, however, is to celebrate in a public space – a website – the students' work, with some of their milestones (they choose which) and their spoken comments.

Conclusion

Examples have been given above of ICT being used creatively as a tool that is integral to the assessment process. Is this the future of assessment? Certainly it is part of the debate that will build such a future. But we can be confident that many more such ambitious explorations are needed if the new opportunities presented by both technology and children's new confidence with it are not to be wasted. Only then can we begin to be certain that the express train of students' capability is not running full tilt at the buffers of the assessment system.

10 Using assessment to improve learning: intentions, feedback and motivation

Gordon Stobart
University of London Institute of Education, London, UK

Introduction

IN CONSIDERING HOW ASSESSMENTS MAY DEVELOP in the future, some of us are particularly concerned with how assessment can be better used in the classroom to improve teaching and learning (assessment *for* learning). Others are involved in improving the assessment *of* learning, in the form of tests or examinations, by utilising the opportunities and the developments that information and communications technology (ICT) are bringing.

These are not approaches that can develop independently of each other. Both are focused on improving learning, particularly those deeper forms that give rise to active and continued interest in learning. They are also interdependent; external tests are not merely neutral indicators of the learning that has taken place – they shape what goes on within the classroom:

> *The [educational] system adjusts its curricular and instructional practices, and students adjust their learning strategies and goals, to maximise scores on tests used to evaluate educational outcomes, and this is particularly true when the stakes are high.*
>
> *(Frederiksen and Collins, 1989, p.27)*

IMPLICATIONS OF RESEARCH FINDINGS

This chapter will explore some of the common ground between effective classroom assessment and developing valid external assessments. It will not set up any false polarities between 'formative' and 'summative' assessment since the same material could be both – the difference is in purpose and timing. The following maxim from Bob Stake (Professor of Education at the University of Illinois) is helpful here: 'When the cook tastes the soup it's formative, when the customer tastes the soup, it's summative'. It is not the purpose of this chapter to tackle the issues of reconciling these different purposes; these have already been well covered by Harlen and James (1997).

Instead, some of the findings from research into effective classroom assessment will be examined and the implications for those developing the next generation of tests and examinations will be considered. This approach should not be construed as raising questions from a position of superior knowledge. All the issues raised are those that continue to exercise those of us seeking to inform teachers' use of assessment for learning.

The assumption is that there is a common agreement that assessment, in whatever form, should aim to foster 'deep learning'. This encourages students to understand underlying principles, so that they can apply this learning in new situations and become active and self-regulated learners outside, as well as inside, the classroom. This certainly appears to fit the philosophy of the World Class Arena tests and other approaches to assessment represented at the 'Whither Assessment?' seminar in March 2002.

The starting point is the Assessment Reform Group's leaflet (2002), which was sent to all schools in England. This offers 10 researched-based principles that are the foundation for effective assessment for learning. This chapter covers three interacting themes, which incorporate most of these principles: learning intentions and success criteria, feedback and motivation.

Learning intentions and success criteria

The term 'learning intentions and success criteria' (borrowed from Shirley Clarke) is used in preference to 'learning *goals* and *assessment* criteria', because it better conveys the emphasis on learning process and on identifying the standard to be reached. The understanding here in terms of assessment for learning is that, for effective learning to take place, both the teacher *and* the student need to be clear about what is to be learned. This is *not* to be confused with task instructions and teaching objectives, which are merely the *vehicle* for this learning.

LEARNING INTENTIONS
In the classroom, students are often not clear about what they are supposed to be learning. Two quotations from Year 10 students illustrate this sense of confusion:

> *It's not that I haven't learnt much. It's just that I don't really understand what I'm doing.*
> *(Harris, Wallace and Rudduck, 1995, p.253)*

> *In my classes I'm in a lot with people who are miles cleverer and teachers only explain it once and I can't follow them. In maths especially like [the teacher] just explains it on the board and I don't understand what he's on about but we've got a book and it explains it as well. So me and my friend are reading through this book because it explains better and by the time we've read it he's on to the next chapter and we don't know what we're doing. We just get lost and everything.*
>
> *(Rudduck, 1996, p.42)*

As adults we have probably encountered that same feeling of lostness when we have asked for help from an ICT 'whizz-kid' who tells us our problem is 'quite simple really'. He then edges us out of the way, takes the keyboard and 'solves' our problem in a flurry of keystrokes – leaving us none the wiser about how to solve it next time.

SUCCESS CRITERIA

For learning to be effective, both teacher and learner need to be clear about what is being learned. What is often the missing link in this process is the need to also be clear on how new learning would be recognised – the success criteria. In classroom assessment, this can be best achieved through negotiation with the students about how they would assess whether the learning intention has been met. This also feeds into self-monitoring and peer assessment, two powerful contributors to effective learning.

The evidence is that in practice we may *identify* success criteria, but we then *assess* using very different criteria (Clarke, 2001). For example, if our intention is to create mood through our writing then the success criteria may be in terms of the reader being able to recognise the particular mood. However, often in classroom assessment, criteria other than those agreed or announced are given pre-eminence, leading to comments that focus on such surface features as neatness and spelling, or other features such as effort and quantity. It is hardly surprising, then, that students often appear confused about what the criteria for good work are – or about the quality of their own work:

> *We did a story and Miss said it was very good – my punctuation and paragraphs.*
>
> *(Year 4 student)*
>
> *Don't know how good it is until it's been marked.*
>
> *(Year 6 student, see University of Bristol, 2000)*

IMPLICATIONS

So what are the implications for those developing external assessments? There may be very similar processes at work – we may intend to assess whether a student has understood a particular topic or mastered a skill but then use a form of assessment that fails to do this. This argument has been powerfully stated by Frederiksen and Collins (1989) in terms of 'systemic validity':

> *… A systemically valid test is one that induces in the education system curricular and instructional changes that foster the development of the cognitive skills that the test is designed to measure.*
>
> *(Frederiksen and Collins, 1989, p.27)*

Their claim is that many of our tests, particularly multiple choice ones, are not valid because in practice they assess and reward very different skills, such as rote learning and test-taking techniques. Garrison Keillor provides a gently absurd example of this in his novel *Lake Wobegon Days*:

> *For years, students of the senior class were required to read ['Phileopolis'] and answer questions about its meaning etc. Teachers were not required to do so, but simply marked according to the correct answers supplied by Miss Quist, including: (1) To extend the benefits of civilization and religion to all peoples, (2) No, (3) Plato, and (4) A wilderness cannot*

satisfy the hunger for beauty and learning, once awakened. The test was the same from year to year, and once the seniors found the answers and passed them to the juniors, nobody read 'Phileopolis' anymore.

(Quoted in Madaus, 1988, p.83)

A more chilling example comes from the study by Gordon and Reese (1997) of the *Texas Assessment of Academic Skills*. From their detailed work with teachers, they concluded that direct teaching to pass the tests can be very effective, so much so that students can pass tests …

… even though [they] have never learned the concepts on which they are being tested. As teachers become more adept at this process, they can even teach students to answer correctly test items intended to measure students' ability to apply, or synthesise, even though the students have not developed application, analysis or synthesis skills.

(Gordon and Reese, 1997, p.364)

Frederiksen and Collins (1989) echo this with their account of a study of a highly successful mathematics teacher whose students did outstandingly well on the geometric reasoning component of New York Regent's College Examination. The study revealed that his approach was to get his students to rote-learn the 12 theorems that the questions were based on, and then 'plug in' the rehearsed learning when they recognised what was being tested. Thus the intended assessment of reasoning ability in geometry was actually rewarding rote learning and test taking techniques. It is likely that this approach is being replicated in most subjects and most test formats.

Just as the classroom teacher is challenged to assess performance in relation to the learning intention, so those developing the next generation of tests will have to attend to the problem of systemic validity. This may raise some difficult issues about the role of the unfamiliar and unexpected in external assessment – so that the best way to prepare is to have a sufficiently deep understanding of the domain or skill to be able to respond to unanticipated questions. This also raises the issue of marking schemes matching the learning intentions, with the distinct possibility that questions may not have correct answers but may have to judge the student's own reasoning.

Feedback

The Assessment Reform Group (ARG) defines assessment for learning as:

the process of seeking and interpreting evidence for use by learners and their teachers to decide where the learners are in their learning, where they need to go and how best to get there.

(ARG, 2002)

One of the key elements in this process is *feedback*, since it is through this that learners can 'close the gap' between current and desired performance.

COMPLEXITIES OF FEEDBACK

What the research evidence is making clear is just how complex the process of feedback in learning is. While we can give feedback that is intended to help the learner to close the gap, this may not necessarily happen. Royce Sadler, in his seminal 1989 article on feedback, comments on

> *the common but puzzling observation that even when teachers provide students with valid and reliable judgments about the quality of their work, improvement does not necessarily follow.*
>
> *(Sadler, 1989, p.119)*

And it is not just that feedback does not improve learning; it may even *interfere* with it. Kluger and DeNisi (1996) conclude from their meta-analysis of the psychological research that:

> *… On about 40 per cent of occasions feedback has negative effects on performance … we believe that researchers and practitioners alike confuse their feelings that feedback is desirable with the question of whether Feedback Intervention benefits performance.*
>
> *(Kluger and DeNisi, 1996, pp.275, 277)*

For feedback in the classroom, which could include performance on external tests, the following play an important role in effective feedback:
* it is clearly linked to the learning intention;
* the learner understands the success criteria/standard;
* it focuses on the *task* rather than the learner (self/ego);
* it gives cues at appropriate levels on how to bridge the gap:
  - self-regulatory/metacognitive;
  - process/deep learning;
  - task /surface learning;
* it challenges, requires action, and is achievable.

The first two bullet points refer back to learning intentions and success criteria, though it is worth noting that Sadler sees the second as critical. Feedback is often ineffective because the learner does not have a shared understanding of what the standard is – and therefore finds it difficult to move towards it. The importance of feedback being on the task rather than the self, bullet point three, is discussed on page 118.

The fourth bullet point needs some de-coding as it is couched in the psychological constructs used by Kluger and DeNisi. The thrust of their argument is that if feedback is pitched at a particular level then the response to it is likely to be at that level. For example, if feedback is in terms of encouraging perseverance with the task ('self-regulation'), the response will be in terms of more effort. While this in itself will not lead to new learning it will provide the context for seeking feedback at the process or task level. Feedback is most powerful when it is provided at the process level and seeks to make connections and grasp underlying principles. Feedback at the task level is productive when it deals with incorrect or partial information, though less so when the task/concept is not understood.

PERILS OF EVALUATIVE FEEDBACK
Research into classroom assessment (Gipps *et al.*, 2000) has shown that even with expert teachers, relatively little of this process- or task-focused 'descriptive' feedback

takes place. Rather, most feedback is 'evaluative' and takes the forms of the teacher signalling approval or disapproval, with judgements about such as the effort made. This is problematic because we know that some of the likely causes of why feedback does *not* improve learning are:

- it does not close the gap (for example, grades/marks; praise/rewards; unclear; too general);
- it is directed at self/ego level rather than the task;
- the learner can choose to:
  - modify the standard;
  - abandon the standard ('retire hurt');
  - reject the feedback/messenger.

The problem with grades, marks and levels is that they do not provide information about how to move forward. For many students they will have a negative effect because:

- learning is likely to stop on the task when a summative grade is awarded for it (Kohn, 1999);
- the level may shift to a self/ego level in which the learners' energies go into reconciling the mark with their view of themselves as learners – what John Hattie calls their 'reputational lens' (Hattie, 2002);
- they may encourage a performance orientation in which the focus is success in relation to others rather than learning.

FEEDBACK AT THE SELF OR EGO LEVEL

The issue around feedback at the self or ego level is that the gap that is to be closed is less to do with learning than with self-perception. If I am given feedback that my work has disappointed my teacher, who knows I could do better, I will seek ways of reconciling these judgements to my own self-understanding. Thus I may attribute the quality of my work to lack of effort, protecting my view of myself as having the ability to do it. However, if the teacher's judgement was on a task I had done my best on I may begin to doubt my ability – a process which if continuously repeated (as it is for many students) may lead to a state of 'learned helplessness' (Dweck, 1986). In this I declare 'I am no good at this' and avoid further exposure to it.

CHOOSING TO USE FEEDBACK

A further, and salutary, factor in feedback not leading to learning is that the learner has a choice as to what to do with this. If 'learners must ultimately be responsible for their learning since no-one else can do it for them' (ARG, 1999, p.7) then how they use feedback is part of this. The risk of only making limited use increases when it is given in the form of a 'gift' – handed over by the giver to the recipient – rather than as part of a dialogue (Askew and Lodge, 2000).

A telling example is how academics deal with feedback they receive on papers they have submitted for publication to journals. If the feedback is that the referees consider that the paper requires substantial changes, which are carefully detailed, before it will be fit for publication, then the author has at least four options:

- to use the feedback to rewrite the article as suggested – this seems to happen after some delay, when the author has 'recovered' from the feedback;

- to 'modify the standard' by seeking out another journal for which acceptance would be less rigorous – and less painful;
- to 'abandon the standard' by declaring that 'my thinking has moved on' – so this is a topic no longer worthy of further effort;
- to 'reject the feedback' on the grounds that the referees had clearly not understood the deep significance of this groundbreaking reconceptualisation etc. – or to declare that it was clear who had refereed this, and this person had been hostile to the author for years …

For those not caught up in this world of academic egos and publications, a similar experience may be that of taking a course for which there is certification at the end. We may start with intentions of getting the highest grade but then modify our standards in the light of disappointing feedback ('all I want to do now is get through'). We may even drop out because we decide we don't now really need this qualification ('abandon') or because it was so badly taught and organised ('reject').

Given these experiences it does not take much empathy with students to see how constant feedback may not always be used to improve learning.

FEEDBACK AND TESTING

Where tests are being used for summative purposes, for example to award a certificate at the end of a course of study, these substantially limit the possibility of providing feedback which will lead to further learning. However the moves towards more detailed profiles of performance allow more opportunity for students to see their relative strengths and weakness. This may help at the self-regulatory level to focus on where further learning may be needed.

However, the more information that is provided, the more feedback there is *for the teacher*, which will allow modifications to be made to future teaching. Anecdotal evidence suggests that while teachers make good use of examiners' reports and other generalised information on performance there is little detailed analysis of their students' performance where scripts are returned to the school (Stobart, 2001). An issue here may be the ease with which weaknesses in answers can be attributed to the particular group of students ('I knew they weren't really concentrating on this'), who have moved on, rather than to the limitations of the teaching. The challenge from this may be to look at how the next generation of ICT-based examinations may be able to provide summary performance data at the school level in a way that highlights strengths and weaknesses in performance and could provide effective feedback on teaching.

The tests of the future may move away from providing one-off final exams. ICT developments make it more likely that 'when ready' testing will become feasible and so tests will have a more formative role in contributing to further learning. Given what we know about what *does* work when giving feedback, this may inform how feedback is given. Though giving grades and marks weakens feedback (Kohn, 1999; Butler, 1988), the reality is that these will be expected. The opportunity is for other forms of feedback to be built in as well – with the advantage that these will be focused on the task and can operate at the process or task level. The challenge will be to provide feedback that allows deep learning (for example, by focusing on the strategy adopted) rather than simply identifying surface features.

Shirley Clarke has observed that a problem area of classroom feedback is that while students are given feedback on a piece of work they are often not required to do anything active with it – so in effect it is ignored. It is particularly unproductive when a comment is made repeatedly (for example, 'You must improve your presentation'). ICT-based testing offers an opportunity to provide feedback cues and to encourage the student to work 'there and then' on performance that has not reached the standard.

Motivation

The roles of motivation in learning and of assessment in motivation are both complex and contentious. Within psychology there are many competing theories of motivation that have been adopted by educationalists (Hidi and Harackiewicz, 2000). At the policy level there are also contentious issues around the role of testing in motivating students and improving learning. The introduction of 'high stakes' national testing in England and state-wide tests in USA as part of the 'standards movement' has led to claims of testing improving both motivation, of teachers as well as of students, and learning. It has also led to opposition from those who see increased testing as undermining the assumptions of lifelong learning and as profoundly demotivating for many students who are most at risk, particularly those from disadvantaged minorities (Orfield and Kornhaber, 2001). The Assessment Reform Group is currently a partner in a systematic review of empirical studies to assess the impact of high stakes testing on motivation.

LEARNING ORIENTATION AND PERFORMANCE ORIENTATION

Some of these polarities are reflected in work on classroom assessment. Here, the emphasis is often on the importance of intrinsic motivation, based on the learners' own drive to learn ('improving competence'). This is contrasted with a 'performance' orientation, with its emphasis on extrinsic motivation that is sustained by rewards and competition ('proving competence'). Table 10.1 on page 121 is an illustration of this polarity, though it is a very oversimplified account – not least in its assumption that intrinsic motivation seems to be a *natural* state rather than one that may have to be nurtured. However, this approach does make some important claims.

Intrinsic (learning) orientation

The first claim is that where there is intrinsic motivation – a desire to learn for the sake of learning – this can be weakened by extrinsic factors such as rewards, or comparison with others. My reading of this is that rewards move any judgements about learning from the learner to an external authority, who takes over as the arbiter of progress. How many of us have found our children absorbed in activity and been unable to resist some 'helpful' coaching – only to find that the children seem to lose interest rapidly and move on to something else, usually something that is *their own*?

Table 10.1: *'How we motivate affects how we learn'*

LEARNING ORIENTATION (INTRINSIC)	PERFORMANCE ORIENTATION (EXTRINSIC)
Belief that effort leads to success	Belief that ability leads to success
Belief in one's ability to learn	Concern to be judged as able, concern to perform
Preference for challenging tasks	Satisfaction from doing better than others
Derives satisfaction from personal success at difficult tasks	Emphasis on normative standards, competition and public evaluation
Uses self-instruction when engaged in task	Helplessness: evaluate self negatively when task is difficult

(Based on Watkins, 2001)

Extrinsic (performance) orientation

The second claim is pertinent to testing policies. Where there is performance orientation, the main concerns are grades and success in relation to other students. If this is encouraged, then students will look for the easiest way to succeed. The skill is then to avoid failure by choosing easier options and becoming a 'cue seeker', looking for the desired response. In terms of feedback levels much of this is operating at the 'self' level, success being measured in terms of public success and attributed to ability. To prevent this view of our ability being undermined by the possibility of poor results we may indulge in 'self-handicapping'. This involves getting ourselves into a situation in which we have a good excuse for not doing well – for example leaving a piece of work so late that it has to be rushed and is therefore 'not up to my normal standard'. (How many of us have stayed up late socialising the night before a key interview or presentation – earning ourselves a good excuse for why we may not have got the job or given a good presentation?) For those who do not do well in this performance-oriented culture, and who come to see it as a consequence of lack of ability, the temptation is, as we saw earlier, to take on 'learned helplessness' (Dweck, 1986).

My concern here is that the testing culture in England will inevitable push us more towards this performance orientation – with an emphasis on results and test taking techniques, rather than on the quality of learning. When the *Daily Mail* becomes alarmed because it estimates that high achieving students may take as many as 105 external tests during their school career ('The exam generation', 26 February 2002) and then the *Times Educational Supplement (TES)* reports on a QCA pilot scheme to award starred grades in national tests for seven year olds (*TES*, 1 March 2002), then we have something to be worried about. If I learn at the age of seven that it's all about getting and maintaining starred grades (for the top one or two per cent) I am in for a performance-oriented school career.

This concern was recently echoed by the director of the Independent Schools Inspectorate (ISI) who said in his 2002 report on private schools' preparation for GCE A levels:

> *Spoonfeeding works. But it works at the risk of something British schools have always been good at: turning out young people able to be inventive, creative, independent-minded, even awkward.*

(Financial Times, 28 February 2002)

121

This is not to argue that *all* extrinsic motivation is wrong, as do some proponents of intrinsic motivation; nevertheless, *overemphasis* on extrinsic motivation distorts how and why we learn. There is increasing evidence that success, which is extrinsically recognised, is a key motivator in learning and may be the first step in the learner beginning to take an intrinsic interest. Hidi and Harackiewicz (2000) concluded, in their meta-analysis on 'motivating the academically unmotivated', that:

> ... *a combination of carefully administered external rewards and situationally interesting activities may be one of the most realistic approaches to educational intervention.*
>
> *(Hidi and Harackiewicz, 2000, p.159)*

LOOKING TO THE FUTURE

Tests may have a role in a learning culture and in motivation. If we are looking to the future of assessment, a better balance needs to be struck than that which is currently in place in England – preferably reducing the focus on using test results for school accountability purposes, as is already happening in Scotland, Wales and Northern Ireland. The possibility of testing 'when ready' so that students can see their learning successes could provide a powerful motivator. So too could allowing students more choice in what they are assessed in and how they are assessed. The ICT developments we are seeing make this a realistic possibility so that we can develop a system of external assessment that will encourage teachers to feel confident and encourage an appetite for learning. This also has implications for the curriculum: '...everything included in a curriculum should be included because it is worth learning for reasons that can be understood' (Brophy, 1998, p.5).

Conclusion

Just as learning intentions, feedback and motivation offer complex challenges in the classroom use of assessment for learning, so they have implications for those involved in developing the next generation of tests – with all the opportunities that developments in ICT may bring. The particular questions this chapter raises are:
- How can we improve validity of our tests so that they encourage the forms of learning we intend?
- How can we develop test regimes that will allow interim feedback which will help learning rather than simply grade it?
- What is an optimal level of external testing if we are to encourage a *learning* rather than a *performance* culture?
- How can developments in assessment be used to encourage more learner choice and autonomy?

11 Formative assessment in action

Christine Harrison
King's College, London, UK

Sue Swaffield
University of Cambridge Faculty of Education, Cambridge, UK

Introduction

FORMATIVE ASSESSMENT, OR ASSESSMENT FOR LEARNING as it is increasingly becoming known, has been shown to improve students' results and promote effective learning. This chapter focuses on the King's Medway Oxfordshire Formative Assessment Project (KMOFAP), which used evidence from a large research base to enhance the quality of teachers' professional practice. The research background and the project are described, along with some general issues that arose. Three of the strategies of formative assessment are then examined; one of these – questioning – is looked at in detail.

'Formative assessment' is taken to refer to all those activities, undertaken by both teachers and students, that provide the information used as feedback to modify the teaching and learning. The research project described concentrates on the detail of formative assessment within the classroom.

Black and Wiliam's research

Professors Paul Black and Dylan Wiliam of King's College London were commissioned to carry out a review of research in classroom assessment by the Assessment Reform Group – a group whose aim is to ensure that public policy at all levels takes account of relevant research in assessment practice. Drawing on 250 journal articles and chapters in books, Black and Wiliam's review was published as 'Assessment and Classroom Learning' in the journal *Assessment in Education* (Black and Wiliam, 1998a), along with other articles responding to the review. The booklet *Inside the Black Box* (Black and Wiliam, 1998b) is a summary of the full review.

In their review of research, Black and Wiliam set out to answer three questions: the responses are described below.

IS THERE EVIDENCE THAT IMPROVING FORMATIVE ASSESSMENT RAISES STANDARDS?

The answer to this first question was an unequivocal 'Yes'. The effect sizes found were between 0.4 and 0.7, which, if related to performance at GCSE, are the equivalent of each student raising his or her results by at least one grade in every subject taken. There was also evidence that lower attaining students were helped even more than others by formative assessment.

IS THERE EVIDENCE THAT THERE IS ROOM FOR IMPROVEMENT?

The answer to the second question was also a clear 'Yes'. Evidence from many sources pointed to the shortcomings of everyday assessment practice. Black and Wiliam discussed these under three headings, which examined:

- those shortcomings concerned with effective learning, or rather the mismatch between assessment practice and effective learning practice;
- those concerned with the negative impact of an overemphasis on grading and comparing students with one another;
- those concerned with the managerial role, as opposed to the learning and teaching role, of much assessment.

IS THERE EVIDENCE ABOUT HOW TO IMPROVE FORMATIVE ASSESSMENT?

The answer to the third question was also in the affirmative, although – as will be explained later – with some hesitation. The response was more of a 'Yes, but ...' The research indicated that improving learning through assessment depends upon five key factors:

> - *the provision of effective feedback to students;*
> - *the active involvement of students in their own learning;*
> - *adjusting teaching to take account of the results of assessment;*
> - *a recognition of the profound influence assessment has on the motivation and self-esteem of students, both of which are crucial influences on learning;*
> - *the need for students to be able to assess themselves and understand how to improve.*
>
> *(Assessment Reform Group, 1999)*

The reason for the qualification in response to the third question was that although the review had provided a detailed analysis of formative assessment strategies, it was also clear that improving practice in classrooms cannot be a straightforward process. Effective formative assessment is not simply a matter of the teacher giving out self-assessment sheets at the end of a unit, or using test results to form teaching groups, for example. True formative assessment involves teachers and students developing a view of learning and teaching within which assessment is embedded. Its effectiveness rests on the belief that everyone has untapped potential for learning. Formative assessment requires that students engage in self-assessment as one means by which they can take responsibility for their learning. Self-assessment should not be seen as 'another hoop to jump through'.

With these considerations in mind, Black and Wiliam argued that there was a need

> ... *to focus on the inside of the 'black box', and so to explore the potential of assessment to raise standards directly as an integral part of each pupil's learning work.*
>
> *(Black and Wiliam, 1998b, p.14)*

As Wiliam put it:

> *We know formative assessment is worth trying. We think we know what it looks like. We don't know how to make it happen in practice.*
>
> *(Wiliam, 1999)*

They therefore set up a project to find out how teachers could be supported in incorporating formative assessment into their classroom practice, not as a 'bolt-on' series of tactics, but integrated into planning and teaching.

The King's Medway Oxfordshire Formative Assessment Project

DESCRIPTION

KMOFAP was funded by the Nuffield Foundation and ran from January 1999 to July 2000, although funding from the United States National Science Foundation and a partnership between King's and Stanford enabled the work to continue after July 2000.

The project involved three secondary schools in each of two local education authorities (LEAs). Of the six schools, four were mixed, one was a boys' school and one a girls' school. The King's team has particular expertise in mathematics and science, and believed that the implications for assessment for learning would be clearer in these subjects than others. KMOFAP therefore concentrated on formative assessment in relation to mathematics and science. To reduce any possible dangers of isolation, two mathematics teachers and two science teachers were identified in each school. The 24 teachers represented a range of expertise and experience: some were young inexperienced teachers, others were established heads of department; some teachers were quite proficient in classroom assessment, some were less competent.

The training consisted of seven and a half days spread over the 18-month period. The teachers would meet the King's team and the two LEA advisers in order to:
- learn about the principles underlying formative assessment;
- develop and refine action plans;
- discuss practice, research and dissemination.

Originally it was planned that some of these meetings would be in the separate LEAs but, as a result of feedback from teachers about the value of working with colleagues from other LEAs, all but one half day were joint meetings in London. Additional local meetings were convened by the LEA advisers. The other form of intervention was visits to schools by project staff, during which teachers were observed and follow-up discussions took place. Some schools also supported KMOFAP teachers by enabling them to observe work in one another's classrooms and giving them time to meet together.

PHASING

There were two main phases to the project. From January to July 1999 the teachers were introduced to the strategies and tactics suggested by the research, and encouraged to experiment with some of them. This informed their creation of action plans, which specified particular classes and formative assessment practices that they would work with during the second phase of the project, from September 1999 to July 2000. The rationale behind starting implementation at the beginning of the academic year was that formative assessment practices involve 'reconstructing the teaching contracts' between the teacher and students (Perrenoud, 1991), and it is easier to do this when establishing ways of working with classes, and meeting new students.

ISSUES ARISING

KMOFAP raised a number of issues, some of which were anticipated and others that were surprising.

Understanding the nature of the research

One of the issues that arose in the early part of the project concerned the teachers' understanding of the nature of the research. Black and Wiliam knew that although their review had made some positive suggestions for the improvement of classroom practice, there was no simple recipe or off-the-shelf solution that could be adopted by all teachers in each of their unique circumstances. Black and Wiliam wanted to avoid the trap of dispensing 'tips for teachers'. The project therefore introduced teachers to the research findings and gave suggestions about directions to explore. Teachers were then given support as they developed and put into practice their own plans.

At first this approach was greeted by some teachers with a frustrated 'Why don't they just tell us what they want us to do?' As Wiliam has expressed it, 'there was a feeling that the researchers were operating with a perverted model of discovery learning' (Wiliam and Lee, 2001, p.2). The resolution of the problem was one example of the invaluable role that the LEA advisers played in KMOFAP. Initially the teachers felt more comfortable expressing their views to the advisers than to the researchers. The LEA advisers listened to and reassured the teachers, and then raised the matter at one of the steering group meetings, so that it could be addressed in future training sessions.

Being observed for discussion, not inspection

It took some time for teachers to feel comfortable with the lesson observations and follow-up discussions. At first, they felt that they were being *inspected* by the researchers who observed their lessons. In the subsequent discussion, questions that were intended by the researcher to encourage reflection were interpreted by some teachers to be further ways of 'testing' them. This was particularly the case when discussing a subject in which the researcher was known to have expertise. When talking about other subjects, questions were more likely to be interpreted as showing genuine interest or enquiry. Despite some initial discomfort with the lesson discussions by a few of the teachers, they all valued them, and were critical when circumstances meant that there was not an adequate opportunity to review an observed lesson.

Drawing on support from headteachers and advisers

As is so often the case, support from the headteacher and leadership team was crucial, in a number of ways. Teachers needed to be released from other commitments so that they could meet the researcher after observed lessons and attend training sessions. Some headteachers also provided greatly appreciated extra release so that project teachers within the same school could meet. At the request of the teachers, the LEA adviser would sometimes organise local project meetings. In schools where the established marking policy was at odds with the practice that KMOFAP teachers were trying (typically where the school required students' work to be graded) the approval and support of the headteacher were required. Dissemination of practice and emerging findings, both within the school and beyond, also required the active support and interest of headteachers.

KEY STRATEGIES IN ASSESSMENT FOR LEARNING

Having explored the general principles of assessment for learning, we now move on to an examination of some key strategies that teachers used in the classroom. It is not possible within the confines of this chapter to do justice to all the strategies that the teachers employed in order to develop their formative practice. However, some pointers are given below concerning questioning (which is examined in detail), feedback and self-assessment.

Questioning

Questions are one of the many assessment tools that teachers use and these might require oral or written answers and be used with individuals, groups of learners or whole classes. A number of different aspects of the questioning process provided a particular challenge to teachers as they considered how best to implement assessment for learning.

- *Evidence of learning:* when teachers ask questions, they seek evidence of learning from the students. The better the questions, the richer the information will be – not only concerning what the students know and understand, but also concerning what they *do not know* or *misunderstand*. The information that teachers obtain from students' answers enables them to make judgements and take action. The more detail that teachers have on what students know, or what the problem is in understanding a part of the work, then the easier it is for them to plan the next learning step. Answers to both written and oral questions contain the clues that teachers need to inform planning and future teaching. For assessment for learning to be effective, therefore, teachers need to focus on creating a rich evidence source from the answers that students give.

- *Whole-class question-and-answer sessions:* whilst it is a useful exercise to analyse learners' written answers to questions, perhaps a more immediate, and often untapped, source of evidence lies in the whole-class question-and-answer sessions that are common practice in most classrooms. These provide a prime site for collecting evidence for assessment for learning. However, there is often an imbalance between

127

teacher and students, with the teacher's voice dominating this part of the lesson. Also, teachers tend to ask low-level recall questions rather than questions that require thought. Recall questions often elicit short, sometimes single-word, answers and so do not provide a rich evidence source for the teacher.

- *Thinking time or 'wait time':* another factor is that the time between a teacher asking a question and taking an answer is often very short. When this time was measured by Mary Budd Rowe in her 1974 study (Rowe, 1974), it was found to have a mean of 0.9 seconds. Such a short period of thinking time or 'wait time' prevents deep thinking by students and so the answers that are given tend to be simple. In these situations, only a small number of students actively take part in trying to answer the teacher's question. Students who have answered one question will often 'switch off' after doing so, recognising that the teacher is trying to involve as many learners as possible in the activity and is therefore unlikely to ask them another question.

The teachers on the KMOFAP project responded to the above challenges with the following results.

- *Framing better questions:* the teachers came to realise that more effort had to be made in framing questions that are worth asking – that is, questions exploring issues that are critical to the students' understanding of the subject matter. They had to set aside time in order to do this effectively.

- *Increasing 'wait time':* the teachers recognised that they had low 'wait times', commonly between one and two seconds. As in Mary Budd Rowe's study, they worked at increasing this time to allow students to formulate fuller and more thoughtful answers. Within a few weeks, they found that this strategy made profound differences to the classroom dialogue. Not only did more students try to answer the questions in class; they also gave answers that were longer and offered more varied ideas. Another outcome was that some students began commenting on the answers of other students, either by elaborating on answers given or by challenging them. This surprised many of the teachers, who realised that students were now listening carefully to what other students were saying and were not 'switching off' or 'waiting for their turn' to answer: instead, they were actively engaging in the classroom discourse.

The KMOFAP teachers described the change that had happened in the question-and-answer sessions as 'changing the rules'. Prior to lengthening wait time, their idea of 'dialogue' in the classroom was that it resembled table tennis. They played skilfully with a few students, firing questions and answers across the classroom. Meanwhile, most other learners were spectators rather than players. Increasing the 'wait time' enabled more students to become players: the pace dropped a little, allowing others to join in. Once the new game was up and running, the questions and answers were used more skilfully. The game began to resemble netball or basketball rather than table tennis. The teacher still had the key position in driving the game forward, but other players (the learners) had a more important role than previously; sometimes they could affect moves forward without the teacher being the instigator. The classroom dialogue had become an interaction between teacher and learners – or between groups of learners, with the teacher listening in. In terms of assessment for learning, this provided teachers not only with a richer source of evidence on which to make judgements, but also with a better vantage point from which to collect the evidence.

Feedback

When KMOFAP teachers began to work on the feedback they gave to students, they looked initially at a number of research studies. The first – by Butler, 1988 – considered how the marking of written work gave opportunities for feedback. Butler's research experiments established that students' learning can be advanced by feedback through comments. The giving of marks, however, is not helpful and, moreover, can have a negative effect: students tend to ignore comments when marks are also given. These results often surprise teachers, but those who have abandoned the giving of marks and grades have found that their experience confirmed the findings: students take note of and act upon comments, which they had previously ignored when grades had accompanied them. However, the precise quality of the feedback is important, as shown in the extensive review of studies of feedback by Kluger and DeNisi (1996). This review found that, whilst the average over all studies showed significant gains, there was a negative effect in about 40 per cent of them. The losses were associated with instances where feedback was merely a judgement or grading and did not indicate how to improve.

Self-assessment

Another area that needs to be developed in assessment for learning is the involvement of the learner in self-assessment strategies. Whilst teachers can help make explicit the gap between where the learners *are now* and where they need to go in their *future* learning (Sadler, 1989), it is the students who must realise what this means and take the appropriate action. Teachers can create opportunities in which learning may take place, but they cannot do the learning. Within the KMOFAP project, a variety of techniques were tried to promote self-assessment; two of the main factors common to all these techniques were the establishment of collaborative group work and the development of peer assessment. It seemed that only when these were functioning at an adequate level in the classroom did the self-assessment begin to work.

ASSESSMENT FOR LEARNING IN ACTION

The following three vignettes provide a flavour of how some of the assessment for learning strategies played out in science lessons. In order to try and glean what assessment for learning means in practice, we suggest that you consider the following three questions as you read each case study:

- How is the teacher collecting evidence to make judgements?
- How is the teacher using judgements to take action to support learning?
- What role do the learners play?

Teacher A

Teacher A taught science in a school for girls aged between 11 and 16 years. She began her work in this area by working on her questioning skills. She used a tape recorder to get an idea of her own 'wait time' during lesson starts and in plenaries. She found that her wait time was between one and two seconds and so she deliberately began to increase it. She found this difficult at first: some of the class became fidgety and so she filled the silence with comments such as, 'I want everyone to think hard on this one,' or ' This is a hard question and so I will just repeat it as you all think up your answers.'

Teacher A also developed her questions so that some of them required careful thought rather than simple recall. She introduced questions like these into her year 7 topic on Forces:

- 'Some people say that slipperiness is the opposite of friction – what do you think?'

- 'Can you describe two or three different ways in which we could find the speed of a skateboarder?'

- 'In the sport of curling, one of the athlete's shoes has a Teflon sole and the other shoe has a sole made of leather. Why do you think the athlete needs different materials on the soles of his shoes?'

She noticed after about three weeks that the class stopped fidgeting during 'wait time' and that more students were offering answers. Also, many of the answers were longer and richer than before.

However, there were still some students who were not attempting to answer questions. Teacher A therefore tried another strategy: when one of the more difficult questions was posed, she asked students to discuss their answers with their neighbours, *before* she asked for an answer from the class. This encouraged more students to offer answers, since they had already had time to articulate and compare their answers with their partners. If the students selected to answer lost their thread or gave vague answers, Teacher A would ask the partners to step in and help.

Teacher B

Teacher B wanted to use assessment for learning in her class to help her students focus on what they had learnt during the lesson and reflect on what they knew and could do at the end of the lesson. She worked with a small class of 12 and 13 year old lower ability students, in which seven of the 16 students had statements of special needs. She had a regular special needs learning assistant to support some of the learners.

At the start of each lesson, Teacher B explained the learning intentions for the lesson and wrote them on one part of the large whiteboard. Sometimes there was one activity planned for each learning intention. Often there were two activities, both on aspects of the same learning intention. At the end of each activity, the teacher stopped and asked the class, 'Which part of today's learning have we just worked on?' She took an answer from one of the more eager boys and then asked another, more reluctant, learner if he agreed. She followed this up with a question about the activity that enabled the second student to show that he had learned something.

In one lesson, for example, a student identified that the first activity had been about learning the parts of a plant cell. A second student agreed that this was correct, and the teacher asked him *how* the learning had taken place. He replied that they had drawn a picture. The teacher asked whether it was possible to know the parts just from a picture. When the boy said 'Yes', several hands shot up around the class. Teacher B told the boy that you needed to *do* something to your picture to show that you knew the parts. She then asked him to pick another student they should ask, to see if he could help. He selected a friend – who told him that you need to put *labels* on the parts. The teacher then asked the class the following questions to check on their learning:

- 'What is the jelly-like material called that fills the inside of the cell?'
- 'What is the tough outer layer called?'
- 'What are the green bits in a plant cell called?'
- 'What do we call the bag of liquid inside a cell?'
- 'What is the round blob called that I told you is like the brain of the cell?'

With each answer she took, she asked a different student to go to the labelled diagram of a plant cell on the whiteboard and point to the appropriate part. Sometimes the students got things wrong because they simply guessed and the teacher would explain that if they did not know an answer they should look for a possible way of finding the answer. Teacher B would tell them that questions in lessons were not like a test and that they could look for help in their exercise books or textbooks, or at what she had written on the whiteboard, or at the posters in the classroom. She also stressed that it was fine to check with others in your group if you were not too sure about the answer.

Around 10 minutes before the end of a lesson, Teacher B generally stopped the class and asked the students to look through their work and think about what they had learned today. This usually required the teacher and the special needs assistant to sit with some groups, encouraging them to do this. After three or four minutes, the teacher asked for a group to volunteer to summarise what they had learned. In the lesson on cells, three of the five groups volunteered and she selected one. She reminded the group that was writing the summary that they could use the learning intentions and diagram of the plant cell and the animal cell that were still on the whiteboard, but she quickly rubbed off the labels on the diagrams. She told the whole class that they could use their books to check on the summary that the group were going to give and also to help them if any questions were asked.

Sometimes the group who wrote the summary simply stated the main parts of the lesson, reading almost word-for-word what they had in their books; on other occasions, the summary group used the occasion to quiz the other groups about what they had done. If the first approach was selected, the teacher tended to ask the rest of the class for a few questions that would test whether the summary group had really absorbed what they claimed to have learned. Sometimes, the summary group remembered things incorrectly, were unable to finish their explanation or matched the wrong learning intention with an activity. In these cases, the rest of the class tended to correct them or to finish off the statement that they had started.

Teacher C

Teacher C wanted to encourage his 15 and 16 year old students to sort out their ideas on plant nutrition. He began by getting the students, in groups of four, to compile poster-size concept maps for the topic. Groups were then split into two pairs. One pair stayed with their poster; the other pair went round the different posters asking the pairs who remained with their poster why they had included some of the terms and why they had linked certain terms together. The pair in each foursome then swapped places. The teacher facilitated a feedback session where students reported on the terminology selected and also on both the good and the confusing links that they had seen. Each time, the teacher probed into the reasoning behind 'good' or 'confusing' links and engaged the students in discussion as to whether certain terms were needed.

Students were then given the following question to discuss:

> *If a villain got hold of a chemical that could destroy chlorophyll, what effect would this have on plants if released?*

Each group of four was asked to write down between three and five criteria that they felt were needed for a good written answer to the question. These criteria were then brainstormed and discussed by the whole class and a final list of criteria was drawn up as follows:
- say what chlorophyll does;
- explain photosynthesis as a process;
- put in the equation for photosynthesis;
- describe the effect on plants of no chlorophyll;
- add any secondary effects that would result from photosynthesis stopping.

Students then wrote their answers for homework. The teacher read their work and wrote comments based on the five criteria. He did not write a grade or mark on this piece of work. Students read the comments and were given time in the next lesson to redraft and improve their answers. When the students had finished, they were encouraged to read one another's answers and to check whether their partner had made the improvements suggested by the teacher. In a few cases, students acted upon the advice of their peers, whilst two students asked the teacher to check through their work again.

Conclusion

Assessment for learning has a vital role to play in the teaching–learning cycle in that it can form an effective means of communication *from* the learners *to* the teacher, as well as vice versa. With better evidence and information about the learning being fed to both teachers and learners, more effective and targeted action can take place. Assessment for learning can begin to drive the learning process.

The KMOFAP project provided the evidence that learning can work in UK classrooms and has provided some of the detail that teachers need to translate the ideas into their own practice. The teachers in this project have been the main agents to its success.

12 Computer-based assessment: a platform for better tests?

Hugh Burkhardt
Mathematics Assessment Resource Service (MARS), University of Nottingham, Nottingham, UK, and School of Education, Michigan State University, Michigan, USA

Daniel Pead
Mathematics Assessment Resource Service (MARS), University of Nottingham, Nottingham, UK

Introduction

THE POTENTIAL OF THE COMPUTER as an aid to better assessment has long been thought exciting but has not yet yielded much that is impressive in practice. Once you look beyond simple short items with multiple-choice or other correct–incorrect response modes, there are difficult and well-understood challenges for assessment designers. Nonetheless, the future looks promising. This chapter will explore, and illustrate with some examples, the opportunities and challenges for the computer as a medium for the four key aspects of assessment: task presentation, student working, student response and evaluating student responses. We shall focus on the domain of problem solving in mathematics, science and design technology.

The chapter is illustrated with examples of tasks, mainly from the World Class Arena project. Static text and pictures are not the ideal medium for describing the interactive experience, so a selection of the tasks discussed is available on the internet at www.nottingham.ac.uk/education/MARS/papers/, under the title of this chapter. Some readers may like to work through the chapter online, trying some of the tasks as they arise.

The role of assessment

Formal assessment, whatever its goals, plays several unavoidable roles, notably:

- *Measuring performance against curriculum goals:* this is the traditional goal of assessment.
- *Epitomising the curriculum:* a set of exemplar tests, preferably with mark schemes and examples of student work, communicate clearly the aspects of performance that will be recognised and rewarded. These may or may not cover the declared objectives of the intended curriculum in a balanced way. For this purpose, assessment tasks are clearer than an analytical curriculum description, and much briefer than a textbook.
- *Driving classroom activities:* for 'high stakes' assessment, where the results have significant consequences for students or teachers, the pattern of classroom learning activities of the *implemented curriculum* will closely match the aspects of performance that appear in the test, that is, the *tested curriculum*. 'What You Test Is What You Get' – hence, 'WYTIWYG'.

Traditionally, public high stakes assessment has downplayed the latter two roles. But the attitude that 'We don't assess that but, of course, all good teachers teach it' provokes weary smiles among hard-pressed teachers, and serious distortions of the education of children. High stakes assessment, if it is to be helpful and benign in its effects, must be a balanced measure of what is important, not just what is easily measurable. Any balanced assessment of the goals of most intended curricula implies the assessment of performance on complex tasks involving higher-level strategic skills and substantial chains of reasoning. In this chapter we focus on such tasks.

The role of computer-based assessment

HOW CAN COMPUTERS HELP?

Before we look in more depth at the challenges and responsibilities of assessment designers, we shall describe some examples that show ways in which computer-based tasks can improve assessment.

First, we think it is worth a brief review of some major features of the history of computer-based assessment. Arising from the mindset of programmers, computers have been used to offer intellectual challenges from the earliest days.

- *1950s:* Early computers offered games, puzzles and 'tests'; compilers were designed to identify errors of syntax, and later of style, in computer programs.
- *1960s:* The creators of learning machines, in which assessment always plays a big part, recognised the value of computers for delivering learning programmes. Nearly all these were linear and branch-free, partly because of the 'combinatorial explosion' that follows when one tries to handle the diversity of errors.
- *1970s:* The huge growth of multiple-choice testing in US education enhanced the attractions of automatic marking, in a self-reinforcing cycle.
- *1980s:* A huge variety of educational software was developed to support learning, with less emphasis on assessment. (Ironically, these materials have not had much impact on the implemented curriculum, but are now a rich source of ideas for high-quality assessment that goes beyond the short item).
- *1990s:* Along with the continuing growth of multiple-choice testing, *integrated learning systems*, a more sophisticated development of the learning machines of the 1960s, began to be taken more seriously.

Since the 1990s, the explosive growth of the internet has begun to raise the possibility that *testing online, on-demand* might replace the traditional 'examination day' model, although many technical and educational challenges remain.

In summary, it is well-established that computer-delivered testing can offer:
- *economies* in the delivery of traditional 'paper' tasks;
- *automatic collection* of student responses *if* they can be expressed as simple alphanumeric text, multiple-choice answers or if they provide some form of positional information, as is the case with 'drag-and-drop' responses;
- *automatic marking* of simple student responses that can be mechanically marked without the need for human judgement or interpretation;
- *new types of task presentation* incorporating interactive multimedia elements.

This makes computers valuable for specific kinds of assessment, which are already delivered via multiple-choice or short-answer papers.

Using computers for multiple-choice or short-answer questions

Figure 12.1: *'Insects' task (for 9 year olds)*

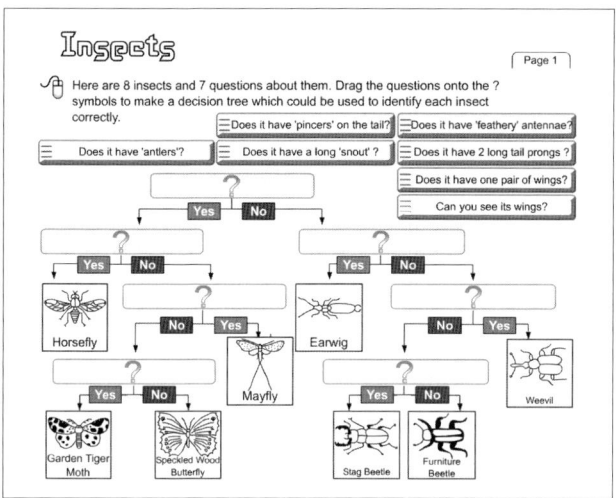

Note: this item, devised by the Mathematics Assessment Resource Service (MARS), 2001 can be tried online at www.nottingham.ac.uk/education/MARS/papers/.

An example of the simple right/wrong approach is 'Insects' (see Figure 12.1, above). This is a classification task, in which students are asked to select appropriate questions for each box on the classification tree from those provided, using drag and drop to input their responses. Essentially a complex multiple-choice task, it suffers from the usual limitations. In this case, it would be more searching to ask the students to *compose* suitable questions. These could be input on the computer but marking them automatically is not straightforward, so there is little or no gain over a paper-based test, and perhaps some loss.

Using computers for more complex questions

The restricted range of task types summarised above should make only a small contribution to any balanced assessment. The major challenges in delivering a wider diversity of assessment via computer include:

- *exploiting the potential of multimedia* and interactivity and meeting the considerable challenges that these present to the task designer;
- *providing a rich and natural working environment* for the student to work on a complex task;
- *collecting richer, more open forms of response* from the student – without turning every assessment into an ICT skills test;
- *marking richer and more open responses* – methods for marking more complex responses based on artificial intelligence (AI) research have been developed, but they face the long-standing unsolved problem of enabling a reliable and defensible interpretation by computers of open responses in natural languages (to which we shall return).

The remaining examples in this chapter show some of our attempts to create more complex, open-ended tasks, which bring in interactive and multimedia elements. Of course, many groups around the world are contributing to this worldwide effort (see Bennett and Persky, 2002, for a rich example).

'Sunflower' (Figure 12.2, below) is an example of a rich genre, an investigative microworld for the student to explore. In this case, it is a simplified simulation of plant growth. The challenge is to find the amounts of the two nutrients, A and B, which will grow the tallest possible sunflower. The computer accepts number pairs and, with a little graphic support, returns the height that would result. This kind of investigation, in which the computer plays a key role, demands a wide range of important skills. Here the student plays the role of scientist.

The reader may like to consider the aspects of performance on this task that they would wish to capture and reward. We shall return to them later, when we discuss human and computer marking of student responses.

Figure 12.2: *'Sunflower' task (for 13 year olds)*

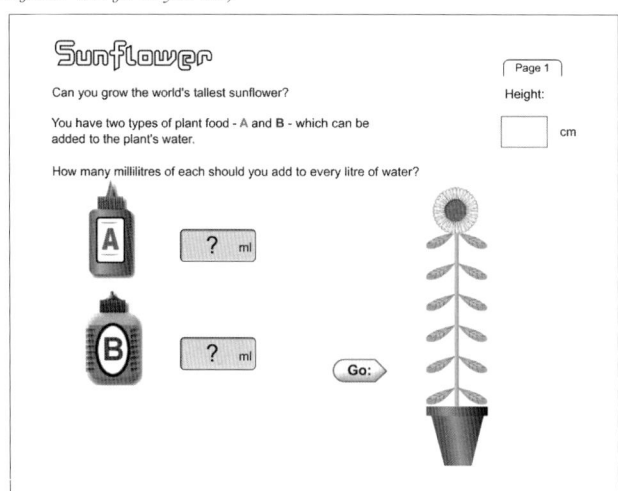

Note: this item, devised by MARS (2001), can be tried online at www.nottingham.ac.uk/education/MARS/papers/.

Figure 12.3: *'Holidays' task (for 9 year olds)*

Holidays

To: Advice@holidayhelp.co.wct
From: bozNkat@klubnet.co.wct

Hi – We need a holiday this August.
Must have great night-life not too far away!
We can afford £400 each – but some spare cash for shopping would be nice.
Help!
Boz & Kat

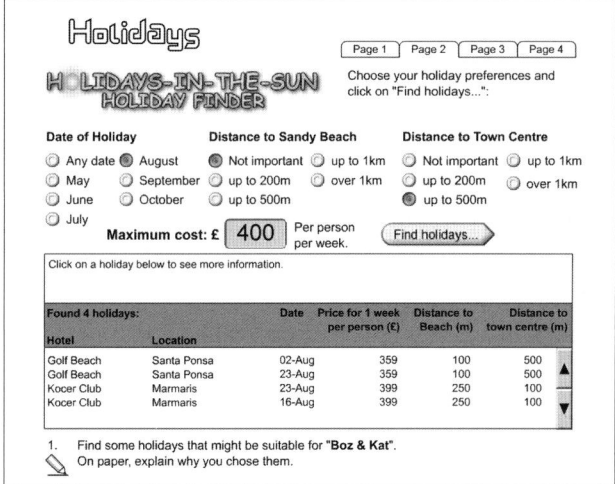

Note: this item, devised by MARS (2001), can be tried online at www.nottingham.ac.uk/education/MARS/papers/.

'Holidays' (Figure 12.3, above) is an example of another rich genre – a task that presents a substantial collection of data, gives the students some constraints, and asks them to make inferences and recommendations. This kind of activity, often based on custom-tailored databases, is both important in real life and a common part of the ICT curriculum in many schools for students from the age of eight years upwards. The level of challenge can be adjusted through the complexity of the task: for example, the number of variables, the nature of the constraints and the richness of the response required, can all be modified. This version asks the student to go beyond numerical factors in the selection of a 'best buy' to take into account other qualitative aspects of the client's requests, and to provide a written explanation of their recommendation. Here the student plays the role of expert consultant.

We shall return to these examples later, as well as introducing others to illustrate specific points. First, we shall comment on some general issues of assessment design.

THE RESPONSIBILITIES OF TEST DESIGNERS

Designers of assessment seek to develop tests that enable students '…to show what they *know, understand* and *can do*' across the domain of the assessment (Cockcroft, 1982). A chapter in the previous book in this series (Burkhardt, 2002) discusses design principles for high-quality balanced assessment that seeks to take this goal seriously; here we shall just summarise some of the key points.

To provide the *opportunity to perform*, any assessment regime should have the properties listed below.

Curriculum balance

Curriculum balance requires that the assessment be fair to all aspects of the intended curriculum. This implies that a teacher who 'teaches to the test' is led to provide a rich and balanced curriculum.

Feedback for teaching and learning

Good feedback is crucial to the effective, self-correcting operation of any dynamic system. In education, a key role of assessment is to provide feedback that is both *formative*, providing guidance for further learning and teaching and *summative*, providing a picture of the students' current level in respect of longer-term goals. In some situations assessment should also be capable of measuring national, and sometimes international, standards, or providing a more detailed diagnostic assessment.

The review by Black and Wiliam (1998b) of research in this area shows the key role that can be played by formative assessment. Selection and accountability tend to dominate discussions of assessment, so that these other constructive roles are often neglected. A better balance would also help counteract the negative view of assessment held by many professionals.

Curriculum value

Curriculum value requires that the assessment tasks should themselves be good learning activities. Tasks such as 'Sunflower' and 'Holidays' both have curriculum value; short assessment items rarely do.

SOME DANGERS IN TEST DESIGN

These responsibilities present great challenges to assessment designers. Much assessment falls far short of meeting, or even of trying to meet, these challenges. Too often, tests consist of rather artificial short items of limited variety. These bear little resemblance to the kinds of task that epitomise the curriculum goals, or which students may meet in real life outside the classroom. This section reviews some of the reasons given for abandoning these goals.

'Good teachers make sure that their students are ready for the test'

The expectation here is that it is the students' responsibility to adapt to the test, and whatever opportunities to perform it may provide – whether or not these cover the learning goals in a balanced way that really allows the students to show what they *know*, *understand* and *can do*.

'Balanced tests cost too much'

It is true that balanced assessment costs more to manage and to mark than short-item tests with right/wrong answers. However, the true cost of assessment is much more than the fee charged for a test. For high stakes assessment, 'test prep' is a major curriculum activity in many classrooms – and for understandable reasons, since careers may depend on the results. Teachers we work with in schools often say 'I've got to stop doing mathematics for six weeks now, and get ready for the test.' Test preparation that does not effectively advance learning of the intended curriculum is part of the cost of assessment (Ridgway, 1999). Thus the real cost of an 'inexpensive' test, which may cost just a dollar per student, but leads to six weeks of otherwise relatively unproductive 'test prep', is hundreds of dollars worth of education time. Hence the need for *curriculum value* in assessment tasks, so that 'test prep' is valuable learning.

'These tests are well-correlated with ... they take less time and are less expensive'

Reliance on correlation as a justification is as commonplace as it is dangerous. It ignores all but the first role of assessment above – performance measurement (see page 134). Once you consider the curriculum effects or the need for formative feedback, the dangers are obvious.

To avoid such pitfalls, high-quality assessment must be in harmony with the curriculum and its goals. We suggest that, when designing assessment, designers should focus on creating a balanced sample of rich, worthwhile tasks, which cover all the dimensions of the domain, along with a modest proportion of short exercise items on other specific skills and concepts.

FOUR KEY ASPECTS OF DESIGN

What implications does all this have for computer-based assessment? We shall now look in more detail at the four key aspects:
- task presentation: will the students understand the task?
- student working: are the tasks set within a natural working environment?
- student response: do students show what they *know, understand*, and *can do*?
- marking: can we assign proper credit from the evidence we collect?

In the light of this analysis, questions that task designers should ask about each task include:
- Is it a worthwhile task?
- What opportunities does it offer the students to show what they can do?
- Does it need the computer?
- Does it need paper?

To answer these questions in each case needs both analysis and holistic judgement.

Task presentation

The analysis here is straightforward. Anything that can be presented on paper can be delivered on screen, though one should ask if there is any gain or loss. In addition there are opportunities for:
- *multimedia presentation*, including video and music that can make the problem clearer and more vivid – without the narrowing that a verbal description always introduces. This can be used for relatively short tasks (for example, 'Speed Limit' – see Figure 12.4 on page 140) but seems to have even greater potential for the presentation of

139

rich open task situations for analysis. Note, however, that there can be practical problems – for example, in a group testing context, headphones are essential to avoid distracting other students.

Figure 12.4: *'Speed Limit' task (for 13 year olds)*

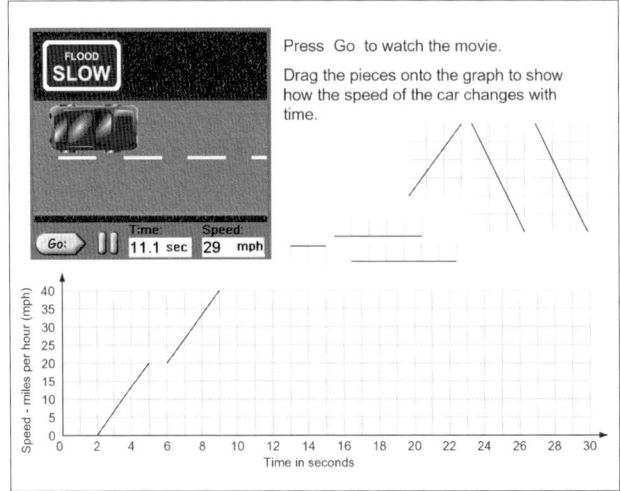

Note: a newer version of this item, devised by MARS (2001), can be tried online at www.nottingham.ac.uk/education/MARS/papers/.

- *rich data* can often be presented on paper but, in assessment as in the real world, custom-tailored computer databases offer opportunities for looking at more data more easily (see 'Holidays', Figure 12.3, page 137).
- *simulations* of practical (or abstract) problem situations for investigation and analysis are a rich and highly promising genre. Examples include 'Sunflower' (see Figure 12.2, page 136) and 'Floaters' (see Figure 12.5, page 141).

One needs, however, to note some negative factors that must be handled by designers:
- *screens hold less information* than a double-page spread on paper, limiting the amount that can be seen at one time. The need to navigate between screens or scroll could cause students to perceive a multi-part task as a series of unrelated items.
- *interactivity can spoil some tasks*: for example, by allowing students to check all their answers, or by encouraging them to persist with trial-and-error searching, rather than think through an analysis. Adapting a conventional task by adding an interactive or multimedia element is liable to cause significant changes in its difficulty and balance.
- *the design and production process becomes far more complex*: facilitating productive interaction between assessment designers, who may have minimal ICT skills, and software developers, who may have no background in education, presents an enormous challenge. Programming aside, the introduction of computers has raised expectations of the standard of graphic design of tests (in World Class Tests this has spilled over to the paper component).

Figure 12.5: *'Floaters' task (for 13 year olds)*

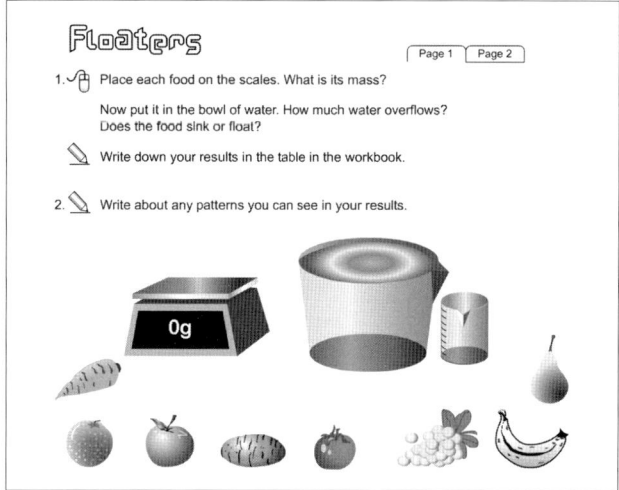

Note: this item, devised by MARS (2001), can be tried online at www.nottingham.ac.uk/education/MARS/papers/.

Student working

We have stressed the importance, if students are to avoid underperformance, of providing an environment for work on each task that is *natural* to them. For computer-based tasks, this is a more difficult matter, since what is natural varies in time and place, according to hardware and software availability and curriculum (or home) experience.

For example, it is not enough to note that students have some experience of word processing; the issue is whether they are used to tackling a particular kind of task in the environment that the test offers – or whether they should be encouraged to, as a matter of policy. Outside schools, so much work is now done on computers that high stakes assessment could be used to drive curriculum, particularly in school subjects other than ICT. However, as always with change, this approach will only work effectively when such pressure is matched with support and funding for curriculum and professional development that enables teachers and students to respond.

In scientific subjects, for example, rough notes and sketching diagrams, graphs and mathematical expressions, play an important part of working on problems. The computer is not yet a natural environment for such working; it is not even clear that it is a good one, at least for a timed assessment. Office-type tools are biased towards presentation of results for 'publication' rather than their development, while software aimed at working scientists takes time and skill to master.

'Bounce' (see Figure 12.6, page 142) is a modelling task, originally presented and tackled on paper. We have also tried it on a spreadsheet with graphing, which seems a good environment for such modeling. Indeed, the output was tidier and more complete *but* the task took an *experienced* spreadsheet user about twice as long to complete as the paper version. A similar effect has been found with other tasks.

Figure 12.6: *'Bounce' task (for 13 year olds)*

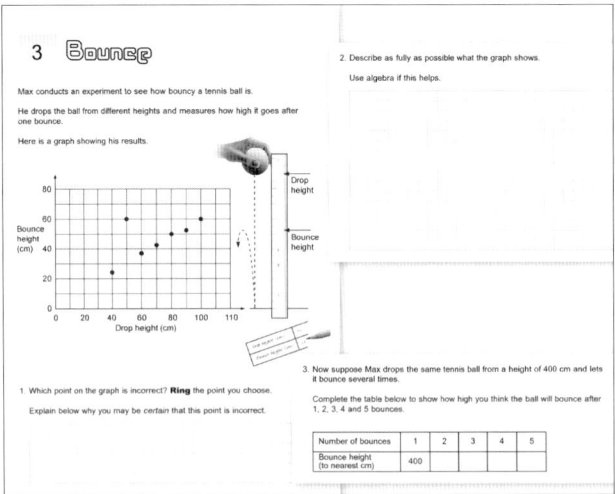

Note: this item was devised by MARS (2001).

There is the further issue of standardisation of software. It is a handicap to be faced with software that is different from that which you regularly use. Even the changes in user interface found between subsequent versions of the same product could pose a distraction on the timescale of a 60-minute test. Possible solutions to this might be:

• Impose *universal user interface standards* on software tools embedded in tests. Students could familiarise themselves with these tools before the test.

• Do not embed the software tools in tests, but *allow students to use external applications* with which they are familiar. This still requires standardisation of data file formats, and presents technical challenges in terms of reliability and prevention of cheating (for example, by accessing calculators or communications tools during tests).

• Ensure that the *user interface of the task is simple enough to learn quickly* (in practice, this should take only a few minutes for timed tests). Most current material takes this approach – with the consequent restriction on types of task and responses discussed earlier.

In summary, and despite these complexities, we have found that the computer can provide a natural working environment, at least for:
• *active investigation of simulated microworlds*: for example, 'Sunflower' (see Figure 12.2, page 136) and 'Make 100' (see Figure 12.7, page 143);
• *exploring rich data sets*: for example, 'Holidays' (see Figure 12.3, page 137) and 'Oxygen' (see Figure 12.8, page 143);
• *natural ICT activities*: as discussed above.

Figure 12.7: *'Make 100' task (for 13 year olds)*

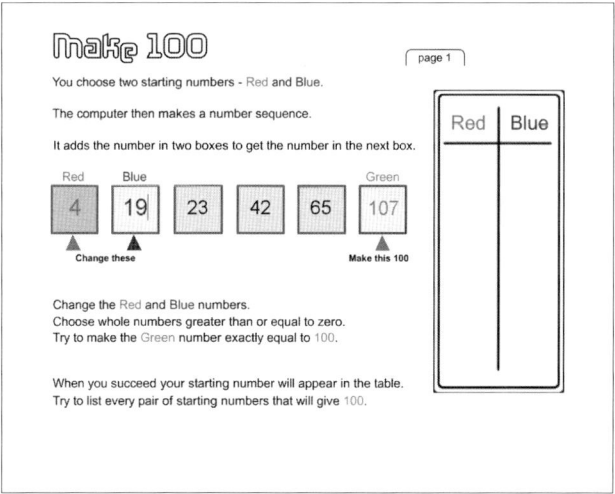

Note: this item, devised by MARS (2001), can be tried online at www.nottingham.ac.uk/education/MARS/papers/.

Figure 12.8: *'Oxygen' task (for 13 year olds)*

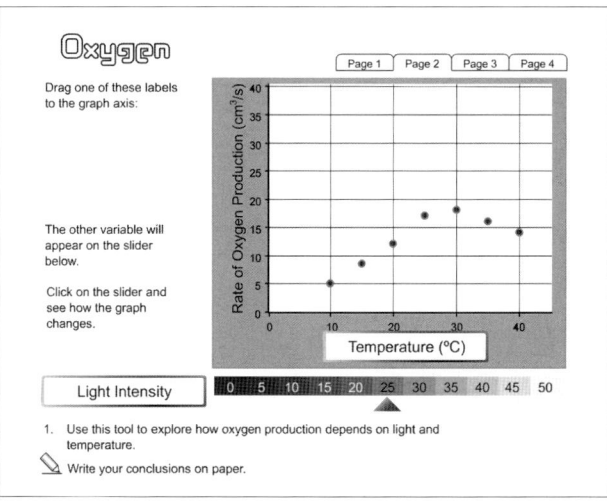

Note: this item, devised by MARS (2001), can be tried online at www.nottingham.ac.uk/education/MARS/papers/.

However, there can be problems arising from:
• time limits on investigation;
• blending computer-based and paper-based work;
• students seeing, and copying, other students' work;
• software familiarity.

Student response

The issues here are closely related to those concerning student working. Indeed it can be argued that, in assessment, the working *is* the response. The following points on the computer's role are important:
• the computer can capture all the interactions of the student with the computer;
• some aspects of the student's work are naturally expressed on the computer;
• the computer provides a natural real-world mode of response to some tasks, though often needing a written response as well.

However:
• only a limited range of the student's thinking is shown through the interactions with the computer;
• it is difficult to capture non-text responses; attempts to do so can spoil a task. For example, in 'Speed Limit' (see Figure 12.4, page 140), though the video presentation of the scene is fine, sketching a graph on paper is a better response mode than dragging the line segments offered onto the graph, which promotes inappropriate multiple-choice thinking;
• the dual mode approach, combining computer-captured and written responses, is often best, but it does not save money – written papers have to be collected, linked to the computer-captured data for that student, and marked by human markers;
• for complex performances, the computer-captured data can be difficult to interpret.

Marking

The core challenge is that, even after 40 years of artificial intelligence, the reliable interpretation by computers of open responses in natural languages is still in general an unsolved problem.

We return to 'Sunflower' (see Figure 12.2, page 136) to give the reader some experience of the kind of challenge that automatic computer-marking represents. For the two nutrients, A and B, the computer captures the successive number-pairs that the student enters, and calculates the resultant height of the sunflower. How far can a computer analysis of only computer-captured responses match human marking with all the information – including, for example, each student's explanation of their approach?

Table 12.1 (see page 145) shows the number pairs tried out by two students working on the 'Sunflower' task; the reader may like to devise an algorithm that will, on the basis of this evidence alone, fairly credit the aspects of performance that we are seeking to assess, namely a systematic search process including, for example:
• controlling the variables, holding one constant;
• trying the combination 0,0 – most plants grow without any added nutrient;
• searching first by orders of magnitude (1, 2, 5, 10, 20 ... not 1, 2, 3, 4 ...);

- going downwards (1, 0.5, 0.2, 0.1, 0.05 ...) as well as upwards;
- systematically homing in on a maximum.

Table 12.2 (see page 146) shows such an algorithm. The reader is invited to judge the extent to which the algorithm is likely to give marks that reflect the elements of performance above. The real test, however, is to compare *computer marks* with *human plus computer marks*, or rank orderings, over a sample of real student responses.

Table 12.1: *Two students' attempts at the 'Sunflower' task (see Figure 12.2)*

STUDENT 1		
Nutrient A (ml)	Nutrient B (ml)	Height (cm)
30	20	0
15	10	0
18	18	0
10	10	0
5	5	0
50	50	0
25	25	0
500	500	0
250	250	0
150	200	0
150	200	0
150	200	0
130	200	0
130	200	0
130	200	0
130	200	0

STUDENT 2		
Nutrient A (ml)	Nutrient B (ml)	Height (cm)
10	0	391.3
0	10	0
5	5	0
10	5	0
15	5	0
15	1	0
15	0	374.8
5	0	325.5
20	0	276.1
20	1	0
7	0	361.7
13	0	391.3
10	0	391.3
11	0	394.6
12	0	394.6
11.5	0	395.0
11.75	0	394.9
11.25	0	394.9
11.4	0	395.0

Table 12.2: *Algorithm designed for the automatic marking of the 'Sunflower' task (see Figure 12.2)*

BEST VALUES OF A AND B	INFERENCE	MARK (TOTAL 6)
$11 \leq A \leq 12$	• Has held B constant. • Has tried 0 or <1 for B. • Has searched for maximum using integers.	+1
$11.0 < A < 12.0$	• Has used decimal fractions.	+1
$0 < B < 1$	• Has used decimal fractions less than 1.	+1
$0.3 \leq B \leq 0.4$	• Shows some sort of systematic search for B. • Has held A constant.	+1
$0.30 < B < 0.40$	• Has gone to 2 decimal places.	+1
$A = 11.5, B = 0.36$	• Full marks!	+1

What *has* been achieved in the field of computer marking of complex responses? Progress has been made in some areas, usually when ambition is more limited. Considerable work is currently being undertaken, in trying to extend the domain of the possible. We shall outline a few examples below.

Marking of computer programming exercises

A system called CourseMaster (originally Ceilidh) was developed by Eric Foxley at the University of Nottingham (see www.cs.nott.ac.uk/CourseMaster/). It provides the students with 'instant' detailed feedback on their submitted coursework, whilst enabling staff to monitor the students, auto-mark their work and generate reports about student plagiarism possibilities. To assess the quality of the programming, it uses test data to provide a (limited) check that the program meets its specification, together with a set of standard algorithms that measure the efficiency of programs. The system is used formatively as well as summatively: to improve their marks, students can revise their programs as often as they like before submitting them for formal assessment.

Marking of short-response items

There are products that attempt semantic analysis of short responses, including checking vocabulary and some syntax. See, for example IAT's AutoMark product (www.intelligentassessment.com/AutoMarkFAQ.htm).

Both CourseMaster and Automark exploit the limited domains of the task type – respectively programming languages, and the limited universe of discourse of a short item. Other computer marking is more ambitious.

Marking of essays

Several marking systems are now available, although they make no attempt at semantic analysis. Rather they assess quality through indirect measures, notably standard readability measures such as sentence length and 'rare' word frequencies. The specialised vocabulary for the essay in question may be 'learnt' by the system through 'training' on samples of good work. Two systems widely used in the US are eRater (go to www.ets.org/research and search for RR-01-03) and Intellimetric (www.intellimetric.com).

However, for any system that ignores meaning, a question arises: 'If you know the marking algorithms, can you fake good answers?' The answer seems to be 'Yes, in principle', though skill is required, and instances seem to be rare in practice. For example, in computer programming, the systematic use of comments that explain the structure is an important feature for enabling program maintenance and later development. Ceilidh checks on this aspect. One student got a good mark, though his (copious) comments consisted entirely of: '/*Blah Blah Blah Blah*/'.

The e-Rater team has conducted a study of this question. They invited a group of experts to write essays that would cheat the system. Some succeeded. The winner just repeated the same (no doubt excellent) paragraph many times (again, see www.ets.org/research and search for RR-01-03).

The other issue facing AI-based marking in high stakes assessment is *defensibility* – can the basis of such results be justified in terms which are accessible to students, parents and potential employers – possibly in the face of appeals over grades?

In view of such concerns and their possible effects, the computer is sometimes used only as a back-up 'second marker'. If the computer mark differs significantly from the human mark, a second human marker is called in. This can still produce important economies in the US context, where there is a tradition of distrust of human marking, and double-marking is therefore common.

FUTURE POSSIBILITIES

We have looked at some of the opportunities and challenges for designers of high-quality computer-based assessment with rich, complex tasks that reflect the major curriculum goals. We finish with a summary of what we regard as the main current opportunities for computer-based assessment to contribute to raising the quality of assessment and, through its influence on the curriculum, of education in schools around the world:

- *simulated microworlds* to be investigated on computer, provide an immensely rich genre in many domains;
- *data-based investigations and modeling* are another rich genre for students of all ages;
- *naturally computer-based tasks*, where the computer is the normal working medium for the student, offer other rich genres, including:
  - spreadsheet-based investigations;
  - text annotation, revision or composition, on word processors;
  - critiquing, modifying and creating designs, on computer-aided design software;
  - computer programming as algorithm design, which reflects a major aspect of modern mathematical thinking patterns;
  - multimedia authoring tasks such as using editing software with video material, either provided or created – see Chapter 9 (Heppell, 2003).

As always, the opportunity for substantial high-quality work is greater when the assessment includes a coursework-portfolio element. The student responses to these tasks will be partly computer-captured and partly written or drawn by hand. The long-mooted shift away from the keyboard towards pen-based user interfaces may help to remove paper from the equation, but does not solve the problems of interpreting the responses. Human marking is likely to predominate, with some computer back-up where this increases efficiency.

In addition there will be some *routine exercises*, which will be entirely computer-handled, including both correct/incorrect response and, increasingly, some AI-based marking of short answers. The proportion of these needs to be modest (say, 20 per cent) in any assessment that purports to reflect the needs of the modern world and the learning goals of most worthwhile curricula.

For the longer term, better AI-based marking of open student responses to rich, complex tasks remains an important area of work but, after 40 years of AI, don't hold your breath. Other work described in this book may make this seem an unambitious agenda, but beware: the history of assessment is full of neat-but-artificial tests that do not reflect the learning goals in a balanced way, and thus undermine the education that society seeks and needs.

References

ASKEW, S. AND LODGE, C. (2000). 'Gifts, ping-pong and loops – linking feedback and learning'. In: ASKEW, S. (Ed.) *Feedback for Learning*. London: Routledge Falmer.

ASSESSMENT REFORM GROUP (1999). *Assessment for Learning: Beyond the Black Box*. Cambridge: Cambridge Institute of Education.

ASSESSMENT REFORM GROUP (2002). *Assessment for Learning: 10 Principles*. Cambridge: Cambridge Institute of Education.

BANDURA, A. (1977). *Social Learning Theory*. Englewood Cliffs, NJ: Prentice-Hall, Inc.

BENNETT, R. E. AND PERSKY, H. (2002). 'Problem solving in technology-rich environments'. In: QUALIFICATIONS AND CURRICULUM AUTHORITY (Ed.) *Assessing Gifted and Talented Children: Papers Presented at an International Seminar, London, February 2001*. London: Qualifications and Curriculum Authority.

BLACK, P. AND WILIAM, D. (1998a). 'Assessment and Classroom Learning.' *Assessment in Education: Principles, Policy and Practice*, 5 (1), 7–74.

BLACK, P. AND WILIAM, D. (1998b). *Inside the Black Box: Raising Standards through Classroom Assessment*. London: King's College School of Education.

BOVILL, E. W. (1962). *English Country Life 1780–1830*. London: Oxford University Press.

BRITISH BROADCASTING CORPORATION AND ULTRALAB (2001). *Generation Xchange Project* (ongoing). London/Chelmsford: BBC and Ultralab.

BROPHY, J. (1998). Towards a model of the value aspects of motivation in education. Unpublished paper presented at American Educational Research Association Annual Meeting, San Diego, USA.

BURKHARDT, H. (2002). 'World Class assessment: principles, practice and problem solving'. In: QUALIFICATIONS AND CURRICULUM AUTHORITY (Ed.) *Assessing Gifted and Talented Children: Papers Presented at an International Seminar, London, February 2001*. London: Qualifications and Curriculum Authority.

BUTLER, R. (1988). 'Enhancing and undermining intrinsic motivation: the effects of task-involving and ego-involving evaluation on interest.' *British Journal of Educational Psychology*, 58, 1–14.

CAZDEN, C. (1988). *Classroom Discourse: The Language of Teaching and Learning*. Portsmouth, New Hampshire: Heinemann.

CITY and GUILDS (2001). *Tomorrow's People – Shaping the Workforce of the Future*. London: The City and Guilds of London Institute.

CLARKE, S. J. (2001). *Unlocking Formative Assessment*. London: Hodder and Stoughton.

COCKROFT REPORT. GREAT BRITAIN. DEPARTMENT OF EDUCATION AND SCIENCE (1982). *Mathematics Counts*. Report of the Committee of Inquiry into the Teaching of Mathematics, London: Her Majesty's Stationery Office.

COLLINS, C. AND ROADS, M. (2002). Internal report compiled for the DfES by QCA. The Use of ICT in Assessment. London: Department for Education and Skills.

COUNCIL FOR THE CURRICULUM, EXAMINATIONS AND ASSESSMENT (2001). *Paperless Examinations Project, Phase 1 Report*. Belfast: CCEA.

CUBAN, L. (1990). 'Reforming again, again, and again.' *Educational Researcher*, 19 (1), 3–13.

DARLING-HAMMOND, L., AND SYKES, G. (Eds) (1999). *Teaching as the Learning Profession: Handbook of Policy and Practice*. San Francisco: Jossey-Bass.

DEWEY, J. (1929). *The Sources of a Science of Education*. New York: Horace Liveright.

DWECK, C.S. (1986). 'Motivational processes affecting learning.' *American Psychologist*, 41, 040–48.

EDGERTON, R. B. (1992). *Sick Societies: Challenging the Myth of Primitive Harmony*. New York: Free Press.

FEIMAN-NEMSER, S. AND FLODEN, R. (1986). 'The cultures of teaching'. In: WITTROCK, M. (Ed.) *Handbook of Research on Teaching (3rd edn.)* (pp.505–26). New York: Macmillan.

FERNANDEZ, C., CHOKSHI, S., CANNON, J., AND YOSHIDA, M. (in press). 'Learning about lesson study in the United States'. In: *New and Old Voices on Japanese Education*. Armonk, New York: M. E. Sharpe.

FORESIGHT: LEARNING IN 2020 TASK FORCE (2001). *The Learning Process in 2020: Point and Click – Learners in the Driving Seat*. London: Department of Trade and Industry.

FREDERIKSEN, J. R., AND COLLINS, A. (1989). 'A systems approach to educational testing.' *Educational Researcher*, 18(9), 27–32.

FULLAN, M. (1991). *The New Meaning of Educational Change*. New York: Teachers College Press.

FULLAN, M. (1993). *Change Forces*. London: Falmer.

GAGE, N. AND BERLINER, D. (1988). *Educational Psychology (4th edn.)* Boston: Houghton Mifflin.

GARET, M.S., PORTER, A.C., DESIMONE, L., BIRMAN, B.F., AND YOON, K.S. (2001). 'What makes professional development effective? Results from a national sample of teachers.' *American Educational Research Journal*, 38, 4, 915–45.

GIPPS, C., MCCALLUM, B. AND HARGREAVES, E. (2000). *What Makes a Good Primary School Teacher? Expert Classroom Strategies*. London: Falmer.

GOLDENBERG, C. N. AND GALLIMORE, R. (1991). 'Local knowledge, research knowledge, and educational change: a case study of early Spanish reading improvement.' *Educational Researcher*, 20 (8), 2–14.

GORDON, S.P. AND REESE, M. (1997). 'High stakes testing: worth the price?' *Journal of School Leadership*, 7, July, 345–68.

GREAT BRITAIN. CABINET OFFICE (1999). *Modernising Government*. (Cm 4310). London: The Stationery Office.

GREAT BRITAIN. DEPARTMENT FOR EDUCATION AND EMPLOYMENT (1998a). Circular no. 4/98. *Requirements for Courses of Initial Teacher Training*. May 1998. London: DfEE.

GREAT BRITAIN. DEPARTMENT FOR EDUCATION AND EMPLOYMENT (1998b). Government Green Paper (Cm 4164). *Teachers: Meeting the Challenge of Change*. December 1998. London: The Stationery Office.

GREAT BRITAIN. DEPARTMENT FOR EDUCATION AND EMPLOYMENT (2001). *Schools Building on Success – Raising Standards, Promoting Diversity, Achieving Results* (Cm 5050). London: The Stationery Office.

GREAT BRITAIN. DEPARTMENT FOR EDUCATION AND SKILLS (2001). Government White Paper. *Schools Achieving Success* (Cm 5230). London: The Stationery Office.

GREAT BRITAIN. DEPARTMENT FOR EDUCATION AND SKILLS (2002). Government Green Paper. 14–19: *Extending Opportunities, Raising Standards* (Cm 5342). February 2002. London: The Stationery Office.

HARGREAVES, D.H. (1998). The knowledge creating school. Unpublished paper presented at the Annual Meetings of the British Educational Research Association, Belfast, Northern Ireland, August.

HARLEN, W. AND JAMES, M. (1997). 'Assessment and learning; differences and relationships between formative and summative assessment.' *Assessment in Education*, 4 (4), 365–79.

HARRIS, S., WALLACE, G. AND RUDDUCK, J. (1995). '"It's not that I haven't learnt much. It's just that I don't really understand what I'm doing": metacognition and secondary school students.' *Research Papers in Education*, 10, 2, 253–71.

HATTIE, J. (2002). The power of feedback for enhancing learning. Personal communication.

HEPPELL, S. (2003). 'Assessment and new technology: new straitjackets or new opportunities?' In: QUALIFICATIONS AND CURRICULUM AUTHORITY (Ed.) *Whither Assessment? Discussions following a Seminar, London, March 2002*. London: Qualifications and Curriculum Authority.

HIDI, S. AND HARACKIEWICZ, J.M. (2000). 'Motivating the academically unmotivated: a critical issue for the twenty-first century.' *Review of Educational Research*, 70, 2, 151–79.

HIEBERT, J., GALLIMORE, R. AND STIGLER, J. (2002). A knowledge base for the teaching profession: what would it look like, and how can we get one? *Educational Researcher* 31, 5, 3–15.

HOETKER, J. AND AHLBRAND, W. (1969). 'The persistence of recitation.' *American Educational Research Journal*, 6, 145–67.

JOHNSTON, D., COX, M. and RHODES, V. (1989). 'The use of word processing in the primary classroom: teacher perceptions and classroom observations'. In: CAL 89 (1989). *Symposium of Computer Assisted Learning*. Oxford: Pergamon Press.

KINGDON, M. (1990). Personal correspondence.

KLUGER, A.V., AND DeNISI, A. (1996). 'The effects of feedback interventions on performance: a historical review, a meta-analysis, and a preliminary feedback intervention theory.' *Psychological Bulletin*, 119, 2, 252–84.

KOHN, A. (1999). *Punished by Rewards: the Trouble with Gold Stars, Incentive Plans, As, Praise and other Bribes*. Boston: Houghton Mifflin.

LAMPERT, M. (2001). *Teaching Problems and the Problems of Teaching*. New Haven, CT: Yale University Press.

LEWIS, C., AND TSUCHIDA, I. (1997). 'Planned educational change in Japan: The shift to student-centered elementary science.' *Journal of Educational Policy*, 12, 313–31.

LEWIS, C., AND TSUCHIDA, I. (1998). 'A lesson is like a swiftly flowing river.' *American Educator*, 22 (4), 12–17; 50–52.

LITTLE, J. AND McLAUGHLIN, M. (Eds.) (1993). *Teachers' Work: Individuals, Colleagues, and Contexts*. New York: Teachers College.

LOUCKS-HORSLEY, S., HEWSON, P. W., LOVE, N., AND STILES, K. E. (1998). *Designing Professional Development for Teachers of Science and Mathematics*. Thousands Oaks, CA: Corwin Press.

MA, L. (1999). *Knowing and Teaching Elementary Mathematics*. Mahwah, NJ: Erlbaum.

MADAUS, G. (1988). 'The influence of testing on the curriculum'. In: TANNER, L. (Ed.) *Critical Issues in Curriculum, 87th Yearbook of the National Society for the Study of Education (NSSE) Part 1*. Chicago: University of Chicago Press.

MUNBY, M., RUSSELL, T. AND MARTIN, A.K. (2001). 'Teachers' knowledge and how it develops'. In: RICHARDSON, V. (Ed.) *Handbook of Research on Teaching* (4th edn., pp.877–904). Washington, DC: American Educational Research Association.

NATIONAL COMMISSION ON MATHEMATICS AND SCIENCE TEACHING FOR THE 21ST CENTURY (2001). *Before It's Too Late: A Report to the Nation*. Washington, DC: Department of Education.

OLDENQUIST, A. (1983). '"Social triage" against Black children.' *American Education*, 19 (4), 12.

ORFIELD, G. AND KORNHABER, M. L. (2001). *Raising Standards or Raising Barriers?* New York: Century Foundation.

OWERS, S. (2002a). *The Place and Perception of Technology in the National Curriculum: Interim Paper*. Chelmsford: Anglia Polytechnic University.

OWERS, S. (2002b). *The Place and Perception of Technology in the National Curriculum*. Chelmsford: Anglia Polytechnic University.

PERRENOUD, P. (1991). 'Towards a pragmatic approach to formative evaluation'. In: WESTON, P. (Ed.) *Assessment of Pupil Achievement: Motivation and School Success*. Amsterdam: Swets and Zeitlinger.

QUALIFICATIONS AND CURRICULUM AUTHORITY (2002a). Summary report of the basic and key skills studies project, prepared for the April 2002 meeting of the basic and key skills project board. Unpublished report.

QUALIFICATIONS AND CURRICULUM AUTHORITY (2002b). Key Skills Qualifications Specification and Guide. London: Qualifications and Curriculum Authority (on behalf of the Northern Ireland Council for the Curriculum, Examinations and Assessment and the Qualifications, Curriculum and Assessment Authority for Wales [ACCAC]).

RICE, J. M. (1893). *The Public School System of the United States*. New York: Century.

RIDGWAY, J. (1999). Personal communication.

ROWE, M. B., (1974). 'Wait time and rewards as instructional variables, their influence on language, logic and fate control.' *Journal of Research in Science Teaching*, 11(2), 81–94.

RUDDUCK, J. (1996). 'Lessons, subjects and the curriculum: issues of "understanding" and "coherence"'. In: RUDDUCK, J., CHAPLAIN, R. AND WALLACE, G. (Eds) *School Improvement: What can Pupils tell us?* (p.42) London: David Fulton.

SADLER, R. (1989). 'Formative assessment and the design of instructional systems.' *Instructional Science*, 18, 119–44.

SARASON, S. B. (1971). *The Culture of the School and the Problem of Change*. Boston: Allyn and Bacon.

SARASON, S. B. (1983). *Schooling in America: Scapegoat and Salvation*. New York: The Free Press.

SARASON, S. B., DAVIDSON, K. S. AND BLATT, B. (1986). *The Preparation of Teachers: an Unstudied Problem in Education* (2nd edn.) Cambridge, MA: Brookline Books.

SAUNDERS, W. AND GOLDENBERG, C. (1996). 'Four primary teachers work to define constructivism and teacher-directed learning: implications for teacher assessment.' *The Elementary School Journal*, 97, 139–61.

SCOTTISH EXAMINATION BOARD (1993). *The Framework for National Testing*. Edinburgh: Scottish Examination Board 5–14 Assessment Unit.

SHANKER, A. (1995). *A National Database of Lessons*. From: *Statement to the US House of Representatives' Committee on Economic and Educational Opportunity*. October, 1995. Reprinted in: *American Educator*, spring/summer 1997, 21, 1 and 2, 35–36.

SHIMAHARA, N. K. (1998). 'The Japanese model of professional development: teaching as craft.' *Teaching and Teacher Education*, 14, 451–62.

SHIMAHARA, N. K. AND SAKAI, A. (1995). *Learning to Teach in Two Cultures: Japan and the United States*. New York: Garland.

SHULMAN, L. S. (1986). 'Those who understand: knowledge growth in teaching.' *Educational Researcher*, 15 (2), 4–14.

SIMON, H. (1957). *Administrative Behavior* (2nd edn.). New York: Macmillan.

STEVENS, R. (1912). *The Question as a Measure of Efficiency in Instruction: a Critical Study of Classroom Practice*. (Contributions to Education No. 48.) New York: Teachers College, Columbia University.

STEVENSON, H.W. AND STIGLER, J.W. (1992). *The Learning Gap: Why our Schools are Failing and What we can Learn from Japanese and Chinese Education*. New York: Simon and Schuster.

STIGLER, J. W., GALLIMORE, R. AND HIEBERT, J. (2000). 'Using video surveys to compare classrooms and teaching across cultures: examples and lessons from the TIMSS video studies.' *Educational Psychologist*, 35, 2, 87–100.

STIGLER, J.W., GONZALES, P., KAWANAKA, T., KNOLL, S. AND SERRANO, A. (1999). *The TIMSS Videotape Classroom Study: Methods and Findings from an Exploratory Research Project on Eighth Grade Mathematics Instruction in Germany, Japan and the United States*. Washington DC: National Center for Education Statistics.

STIGLER, J. W. AND HIEBERT, J. (1999). *The Teaching Gap: Best Ideas from the World's Teachers for Improving Education in the Classroom*. New York: Free Press.

STOBART, G. (2001). 'The validity of national curriculum assessment.' *British Journal of Educational Studies*, 49, 1, 26–39.

THARP, R. G. AND GALLIMORE, R. (1989). *Rousing Minds to Life: Teaching, Learning, and Schooling in Social Context*. Cambridge: Cambridge University Press.

THORNDIKE, R.L., HAGEN, E. AND FRANCE, N. (2001). *Cognitive Abilities Test (3rd edn.)* Windsor: NFER-NELSON.

UNIVERSITY OF BRISTOL – CLIO CENTRE FOR ASSESSMENT STUDIES (2000). *The LEARN Project: Guidance for Schools on Assessment for Learning. Report prepared for QCA*.

WAGNER, T. (1994). *How Schools Change*. Boston, Massachusetts: Beacon.

WATKINS, C. (2001). 'Learning about learning improves performance.' *National School Improvement Network (NSIN) Research Matters*, 13, 1–8. London: Institute of Education.

References

WILIAM, D. (1999). KMOFAP training session at King's College London, 4 February 1999.

WILIAM, D. AND LEE, C. (2001). Teachers developing assessment for learning: impact on pupil achievement. Paper presented at British Educational Research Association 27th Annual Conference held at the University of Leeds, September 2001.

YINGER, R. (1999). 'The role of standards in teaching and teacher education'. In: GRIFFIN, G. (Ed.) *The Education of Teachers: Ninety-eighth Yearbook of the National Society for the Study of Education* (pp.85–113). Chicago, Illinois: University of Chicago Press.

YOSHIDA, M. (1999). Lesson study: an ethnographic investigation of school-based teacher development in Japan. Doctoral dissertation, University of Chicago.

154

Index

Also available from QCA

Assessing Gifted and Talented Children
Compiled and edited by Carolyn Richardson

In developing international tests and support materials for the
World Class Arena, QCA is in contact with teachers and experts
in gifted and talented education from all over the world. In
February 2001, it hosted an international seminar on the subject,
comprising several days of lively discussion and informative
presentations. This book is based on nine of those presentations.

Assessing Gifted and Talented Children provides an
international view on how these students can best be identified.
It gives information on current provision in the USA, Australia and
the UK and will provide policymakers and educationalists around
the world with a stimulating insight into how the talents of gifted
students may be nurtured and developed.

Provision for the gifted will not only create new opportunities
for the most able; it will also improve learning and achievement
for all students, providing new motivation and challenging minds.

ISBN 1 85838 490 7